First World War
and Army of Occupation
War Diary
France, Belgium and Germany

3 CAVALRY DIVISION
Divisional Troops
Royal Army Service Corps
Divisional Ammunition Park (76 Company A.S.C.)
1 February 1915 - 31 October 1917

WO95/1151/2

The Naval & Military Press Ltd
www.nmarchive.com
Published in association with The National Archives

Published by

The Naval & Military Press Ltd

Unit 10 Ridgewood Industrial Park,

Uckfield, East Sussex,

TN22 5QE England

Tel: +44 (0) 1825 749494

www.naval-military-press.com

www.nmarchive.com

This diary has been reprinted in facsimile from the original. Any imperfections are inevitably reproduced and the quality may fall short of modern type and cartographic standards.

© **Crown Copyright**
Images reproduced by permission of The National Archives, London, England, 2015.

Contents

Document type	Place/Title	Date From	Date To
Heading	WO95/1151/2		
Heading	3rd Cav Div Troops 3rd Cav Div Amms Park (76 Coy ASC) 1915 Feb-1917 Oct To GHQ Troops Box 135		
Heading	3rd Cav Div Troops War Diary of 3rd Cavalry Ammunition Park From 1st February 1915 To 28th February 1915 Volume I (76 Co ASC) To Sept. 1917		
War Diary	Morbecque	01/02/1915	28/02/1915
Heading	War Diary of 3rd Cavalry Ammunition Park From March 1st 1915 To March 31st 1915 (Volume 2)		
War Diary	Morbecque	01/03/1915	31/03/1915
Heading	War Diary of 3rd Cavalry Ammunition Park From 1st April 1915 To 30th April 1915 (Volume 3)		
War Diary	Morbecque	01/04/1915	30/04/1915
Heading	3rd Cavalry Division War Diary of 3rd Cav Amm Park From 1st May 1915 To 31st May 1915 (Volume 4)		
War Diary	Morbecque	01/05/1915	31/05/1915
Heading	3rd Cavalry Division War Diary of 3rd Cav Amm Park From 1st June 1915 To 30th June 1915 (Volume 5)		
War Diary	Morbecque	01/06/1915	29/06/1915
Heading	3rd Cavalry Division War Diary of 3rd Cav Ammunition Park From 1st July 1915 To 31st July 1915 (Volume 6)		
War Diary	Morbecque	01/07/1915	31/07/1915
Heading	3rd Cavalry Division War Diary of3rd Cav. Amm Park. From 1st August 1915 To 31st August 1915 (Volume 7)		
War Diary	Morbecque	01/08/1915	04/08/1915
War Diary	Enquin Les Mines.	05/08/1915	31/08/1915
War Diary		16/08/1915	16/08/1915
Heading	3rd Cavalry Division War Diary of 3rd Cav. Ammunition Park. From 1st September 1915 To 30th September 1915 (Volume 8)		
War Diary	Enquin Les Mines	01/09/1915	22/09/1915
War Diary	Auchel	23/09/1915	25/09/1915
War Diary	W.O.C.	26/09/1915	26/09/1915
War Diary	Auchel	27/09/1915	30/09/1915
War Diary	Enquin Les Mines	06/09/1915	24/09/1915
War Diary	Auchel	24/09/1915	29/09/1915
War Diary	Enquin Les Mines	14/09/1915	21/09/1915
War Diary	Auchel	25/09/1915	30/09/1915
Heading	3rd Cavalry Division No. 3 Cav. Ammn. Park Oct. 15 Vol IX		
Heading	War Diary of 3rd Cav Ammunition Park From 1st Oct 1915 To 31st Oct 1915 (Volume 9)		
War Diary	Auchel	01/10/1915	05/10/1915
War Diary	Auchel	06/09/1915	19/09/1915
War Diary	Lambres	22/09/1915	31/09/1915
War Diary	Auchel	01/10/1915	25/10/1915
War Diary		14/10/1915	15/10/1915
War Diary	Lambres	25/10/1915	29/10/1915

Heading	3rd Cavalry Division War Diary of 3rd Cavalry Ammunition Park From 1st Nov. 1915 To 30th Nov. 1915 (Volume 10)		
War Diary	Lambres	01/11/1915	17/11/1915
War Diary	Fruges	18/11/1915	30/11/1915
War Diary		01/11/1915	29/11/1915
Heading	War Diary of 3rd Cavalry. Ammunition Park From 1st Dec. 1915 To 31st Dec. 1915 (Volume XI)		
War Diary	Fruges	01/12/1915	31/12/1915
War Diary	Fruges	02/12/1915	30/12/1915
Heading	War Diary of 3rd Cavalry Ammunition Park From 1st January 1916 To 31st January 1916 (Volume 12)		
War Diary	Letailly	01/01/1916	31/01/1916
War Diary	Letailly	05/01/1916	31/01/1916
Heading	War Diary of 3rd Cavalry Ammunition Park. From 1st Feb. 1916 To 29 Feb. 1916 (Volume. 13)		
War Diary	Letailly	01/02/1916	20/02/1916
War Diary	Fruges	22/02/1916	29/02/1916
War Diary	Fruges	10/02/1916	25/02/1916
Heading	War Diary of 3rd Cavalry Ammunition Park From 1st March 1916 To 31st March 1916 (Volume 14)		
War Diary	Fruges	01/03/1916	31/03/1916
War Diary	Fruges	01/03/1916	27/03/1916
Heading	War Diary of 3rd Cavalry Ammunition Park. From 1st April 1916 To 30th April 1916 (Volume 15)		
War Diary	Fruges	01/04/1916	30/04/1916
War Diary		03/04/1916	14/04/1916
Heading	War Diary of 3rd Cavalry Ammunition Park From 1st May 1916 To 31st May 1916 (Volume 16)		
War Diary	Fruges	01/05/1916	31/05/1916
War Diary	Fruges.	01/05/1916	26/05/1916
Heading	3c L8c Vol 17 Confidential War Diary of 3rd Cavalry Ammunition Park. From 1st June. 1916 To 30th June. 1916 (Volume 17)		
War Diary	Fruges	01/06/1916	25/06/1916
War Diary	Domart	26/06/1916	26/06/1916
War Diary	Laneuville	27/06/1916	29/06/1916
War Diary	O L Contay	29/06/1916	29/06/1916
Heading	War Diary of 3rd Cavalry Ammunition Park. From 1st July 1916 To 31st July 1916 (Volume 18)		
War Diary	Hallencourt	04/07/1916	13/07/1916
War Diary	Laneuville	14/07/1916	30/07/1916
War Diary	O L Contay	15/07/1916	29/07/1916
Heading	War Diary of 3rd Cavalry Ammunition Parks. From 1st August 1916 To 31st August 1916 (Volume 19)		
War Diary	Laneuville	01/08/1916	01/08/1916
War Diary	Argenvillers	02/08/1916	03/08/1916
War Diary	Fruges	04/08/1916	31/08/1916
War Diary	Field	12/08/1916	25/08/1916
Heading	War Diary of 3rd Cavalry Ammunition Park From 1st September 1916 To 30th September 1916 (Volume 20)		
War Diary	Fruges	04/09/1916	10/09/1916
War Diary	Gueschart	11/09/1916	11/09/1916
War Diary	Belloy Sur Somme	12/09/1916	13/09/1916
War Diary	Bussy Les Daours-Allonville Road. 62 D H 25 a 79	14/09/1916	15/09/1916
War Diary	62 D H 25 a 79	18/09/1916	21/09/1916

War Diary	Villers L'Hopital	23/09/1916	23/09/1916
War Diary	Hauteville	24/09/1916	30/09/1916
War Diary	O L Contay	14/09/1916	15/09/1916
War Diary	O O Boulogne	04/09/1916	08/09/1916
War Diary	O C Bdes	10/09/1916	10/09/1916
War Diary	O L Contay	14/09/1916	20/09/1916
War Diary	O O Boulogne	04/09/1916	08/09/1916
War Diary	O O Boulogne	04/09/1916	04/09/1916
War Diary	O C Bdes	10/09/1916	10/09/1916
War Diary	O L Contay	14/09/1916	14/09/1916
War Diary	O O Boulogne	04/09/1916	04/09/1916
War Diary	O C Bdes	10/09/1916	10/09/1916
War Diary	O L Contay	19/09/1916	19/09/1916
War Diary	AA & QMG	17/09/1916	17/09/1916
Heading	War Diary of 3rd Cavalry Ammunition Park. From 1st October 1916 To 31st October 1916 (Volume 21)		
War Diary	Hauteville	01/10/1916	20/10/1916
War Diary	Wailly	21/10/1916	31/10/1916
War Diary	Campigneules Les Petites	31/10/1916	31/10/1916
War Diary	O E Argues	10/10/1916	14/10/1916
War Diary	O O Boulogne	22/10/1916	22/10/1916
War Diary	O E Argues	10/10/1916	14/10/1916
War Diary	O O Boulogne	22/10/1916	22/10/1916
War Diary	O O Boulogne	04/10/1916	04/10/1916
Heading	War Diary of 3rd Cavalry Ammunition Park From 1st November 1916 To 30th November 1916 Volume 22		
War Diary	Campigneules Les Petites	01/11/1916	30/11/1916
War Diary	O C	25/11/1916	25/11/1916
Heading	War Diary of 3rd Cavalry Ammunition Park From 1st December 1916 To 31st December 1916 (Volume 23)		
War Diary	Campigneules Les Petites	02/12/1916	30/12/1916
War Diary	O O Boulogne	12/12/1916	31/12/1916
War Diary	O D Heden	05/12/1916	05/12/1916
War Diary	O C Amlool	09/12/1916	29/12/1916
War Diary	O C yih Light	22/12/1916	22/12/1916
War Diary	O C Regements	06/12/1916	06/12/1916
Heading	War Diary of 3rd Cavalry Ammunition Park. From 1st January 1917 To 31st January 1917 (Volume 24)		
War Diary	Campigneules Les Petites	01/01/1917	18/01/1917
War Diary	Campigneules	19/01/1917	24/01/1917
War Diary	Campigneules Les Petites	25/01/1917	31/01/1917
Heading	War Diary of 3rd Cavalry Ammunition Park From 1st February 1917 To 28th February 1917 (Volume 25)		
War Diary	Campigneules Les Petites	01/02/1917	28/02/1917
War Diary	O C am Col	13/02/1917	18/02/1917
War Diary	O C am Col	15/02/1917	18/02/1917
War Diary	S a a. 303 Ball	06/02/1917	23/02/1917
War Diary	Gounales mills no 5 O.C 7th Z.a les my	03/02/1917	03/02/1917
Heading	War Diary of 3rd Cavalry Ammunition Park. From 1st March 1917 To March 31st 1917 (Volume 26)		
War Diary	Campigneules Les Petites	01/03/1917	31/03/1917
War Diary	Q 7 13th Shrapinel	10/03/1917	27/03/1917
War Diary	Q.7 13 Pr A.E	10/03/1917	23/03/1917
War Diary	3 Pr A.F	26/03/1917	26/03/1917
Heading	War Diary of 3rd Cavalry Ammunition Park From 1st April 1917 To 30th April 30th (Volume 27)		

War Diary	Campigneules Les Petites	01/04/1917	06/04/1917
War Diary	La Brique Terie	07/04/1917	07/04/1917
War Diary	Ligny St Flochel	08/04/1917	19/04/1917
War Diary	Regnauville	20/04/1917	30/04/1917
War Diary	OO Savy Q7 Pr Sharpnil	08/04/1917	08/04/1917
War Diary	OC A H J Coy 3 Cav Div Shrapnil	23/04/1917	23/04/1917
War Diary	OC Am Col 3 Cav Div Shrapnil	28/03/1917	28/03/1917
War Diary	OC "K" Bty RHA Shrapnil	28/03/1917	28/03/1917
War Diary	OO Savy Q7 13 Pr Shrapnil.	08/04/1917	08/04/1917
War Diary	OC A H J Coy 3rd Coy Div Shrapnil	23/04/1917	23/04/1917
War Diary	OC Am Col 3rd Cav Div Shrapnil	28/03/1917	28/04/1917
War Diary	OC "K" Bty RHA Shrapnil	28/04/1917	28/04/1917
War Diary	OC A.F.J Coy 3rd. Cav Div SAA.	11/04/1917	11/04/1917
War Diary	OO Savye 3 Pr A.F.E.	08/04/1917	08/04/1917
War Diary	A H J Coy 3rd Cav Div Q7 13 Pr Sharpnil	08/04/1917	08/04/1917
War Diary	OC Am Col 3rd Cav Div Q7 13 Pr	28/04/1917	28/04/1917
War Diary	OC "K" Bty RHA Q7 13 Pr	28/04/1917	28/04/1917
War Diary	OC AHJ Coy 3rd Cav Div H.E.	08/04/1917	08/04/1917
War Diary	OC AM Col 3rd Cav Div	28/04/1917	28/04/1917
War Diary	OC "K" Bty RHA	28/04/1917	28/04/1917
War Diary	OC AHJ Coy 3rd Cav Div SAA	08/04/1917	08/04/1917
War Diary	OC Savy SAA	11/04/1917	11/04/1917
War Diary	OC Savy 3 Pr AF. E	11/04/1917	11/04/1917
War Diary	OC Am Col 3rd SAA	24/04/1917	24/04/1917
War Diary	OC 10th Royal Hussars SAA	25/04/1917	25/04/1917
War Diary	OC NS Yeo SAA	26/04/1917	26/04/1917
War Diary	OC Am Col 3rd Cav Div SAA	27/04/1917	27/04/1917
War Diary	OC Royal Horse Guards SAA	27/04/1917	27/04/1917
Heading	War Diary of 3rd Cavalry Ammunition Park From 1st May 1917 To 31st May 1917 (Volume 28)		
War Diary	Regnauville	01/05/1917	18/05/1917
War Diary	Villers Bocage	19/05/1917	19/05/1917
War Diary	Villers Carbonnel	20/05/1917	21/05/1917
War Diary	Tincourt	22/05/1917	29/05/1917
War Diary	Bray-Sur-Somme	30/05/1917	30/05/1917
Miscellaneous	O C Essex Yeomanry	01/05/1917	01/05/1917
War Diary	O C 10th Royal Hussars S.A.A. "303	02/05/1917	02/05/1917
War Diary	O C 10th Royal Hussars Webley Pistol	02/05/1917	02/05/1917
War Diary	O C 3rd Dragoon Guards. S.A.A. 303	02/05/1917	02/05/1917
War Diary	O C 3rd Cav amm Column S.A.A. 303	06/05/1917	06/05/1917
War Diary	O C 3rd Cav amm Column. Pestol Welley	06/05/1917	06/05/1917
War Diary	O C 8th M.G. Squadron Pestol Welley	06/05/1917	06/05/1917
War Diary	O C 8th M.G. Squadron S.A.A. 303	06/05/1917	06/05/1917
War Diary	O C. Cly Bty R.H.A. S.A.A. 303	07/05/1917	07/05/1917
War Diary	O C. Bty R.H.A. S.A.A. Pistol Webley	07/05/1917	07/05/1917
War Diary	O O Dannes SAA 303	11/05/1917	11/05/1917
War Diary	O C 8th M.Y Squadron. SAA "303	11/05/1917	11/05/1917
War Diary	O O Dannes N	11/05/1917	11/05/1917
War Diary	O O 8th M.G. Squadron SAA 303	11/05/1917	11/05/1917
War Diary	O O Dannes Defective Rounds	11/05/1917	11/05/1917
War Diary	D.A. DOS SAA. 303	11/05/1917	11/05/1917
War Diary	O C am: Col.3rd Cav Div Cont: Flam:1"	12/05/1917	12/05/1917
War Diary	O C am: Res Park N.	23/05/1917	23/05/1917
War Diary	O C am: Res Park N X		
War Diary	O C. Essex Yeomanry Mills No 5	24/05/1917	24/05/1917
War Diary	O C. Royal Horse Yds mill No	21/05/1917	21/05/1917

War Diary	O C. 4th Bde am: Col MIl Mills No 5	21/05/1917	21/05/1917
Miscellaneous	War Diary of 3rd Cavalry Ammunition Park. From 1st June 1917 To 30th June 1917 (Volume 29)		
War Diary	Bray-Sur Somme	01/06/1917	30/06/1917
War Diary		00/06/1917	00/06/1917
Heading	War Diary of 3rd Cavalry Ammunition Park From 1st July 1917 To 31st July 1917 Volume 30		
War Diary	Le Mesnil	01/07/1917	15/07/1917
War Diary	Pernes	16/07/1917	17/07/1917
War Diary	Hollanderie	18/07/1917	31/07/1917
War Diary	Q. 7	15/07/1917	15/07/1917
War Diary	O.C. "K" Bty Rha N	25/07/1916	25/07/1916
War Diary	O.C. "C" Bty Rha N	26/07/1916	26/07/1916
War Diary	Q.7.13. N	30/07/1916	30/07/1916
Heading	War Diary of 3rd Cavalry Ammunition Park From 1st August 1917 To 31st August 1917 Volume 31		
War Diary	Hollanderie	01/08/1917	31/08/1917
War Diary	S a a 303 Ball	02/08/1917	02/08/1917
War Diary	Cart. Illam 1"	02/08/1917	02/08/1917
War Diary	Green Flares no 3	02/08/1917	02/08/1917
War Diary	Pistol Webley	02/08/1917	02/08/1917
War Diary	Green Flares no 3	12/08/1917	12/08/1917
War Diary	Shrapnel N Peselhoek	18/08/1917	18/08/1917
War Diary	S a a 303 7th M G Sqadn	22/08/1917	22/08/1917
War Diary	S a a 303 Arras	27/08/1917	27/08/1917
War Diary	S a a 303 O.C. Sary yeo	02/08/1917	02/08/1917
War Diary	S a a 303 O.C ammrn: Col	02/08/1917	11/08/1917
War Diary	Pistol Webley	02/08/1917	02/08/1917
War Diary	Shrapnel N 5th Cav am Col	17/08/1917	17/08/1917
War Diary	S a a 303 am Col	25/08/1917	27/08/1917
Heading	War Diary of 3rd Cavalry Ammunition Park. From 1st September 1917 To 30th September 1917 Volume 32		
Miscellaneous	Mileage and Petrol Consumption for September 1917		
War Diary	Hollandrie	01/09/1917	30/09/1917
War Diary	O C Ammn Col S a a "303	03/09/1917	25/09/1917
War Diary	O C "G" Battry Rna N	27/09/1917	27/09/1917
War Diary	O C 7th M G Squadn. S A A 303	03/09/1917	03/09/1917
War Diary	O C 1st life Guards S A A 303	03/09/1917	03/09/1917
War Diary	O C Leices Yeo SAA 303	08/09/1917	08/09/1917
War Diary	O C 7 Escort Squdn S A A 303	09/09/1917	09/09/1917
War Diary	O C 7 Escort Squdn Pistol Webley	09/09/1917	09/09/1917
War Diary	O C "K" Battery R H A N Shrapnil	26/09/1917	26/09/1917
War Diary	O C "K" Battery R H A Nx A.E.	26/09/1917	26/09/1917
War Diary	O C 2nd Life Guards S A A 303	26/09/1917	26/09/1917
War Diary	O C "K" Battery R H A N Shrapnil	27/09/1917	27/09/1917
Heading	War Diary of 76th Company A.S.C. (M.T.) From 1st October 1917 To 31st October 1917 Volume 33		
War Diary	Hollandrie	01/10/1917	21/10/1917
War Diary	Abbeyville	22/10/1917	23/10/1917
War Diary	St Valery Sur Somme	24/10/1917	31/10/1917

WO 95/1151/2

3rd CAV DIV TROOPS

3rd Cav Div Ammo Park
(76 Coy ASC)

1915 FEB — 1917 ~~OCT~~

TO GHQ TROOPS
BOX 135 ~~Ammo Box~~

$\frac{121}{4812}$

Confidential

War Diary
of
2nd Cavalry Ammunition Park.

From 1st February 1915   To 28th February 1915

Volume III

Army Form C. 2118.

WAR DIARY
~~INTELLIGENCE~~ SUMMARY

(Erase heading not required.)

Instructions regarding War Diaries and Intelligence Summaries are contained in F. S. Regs, Part II. and the Staff Manual respectively. Title pages will be prepared in manuscript.

Hour, Date, Place	Summary of Events and Information	Remarks and references to Appendices
MORBECQUE 1st	24,000 rds S.A.A. issued to 1st Royal Dragoons	Ent
" 2nd	2 lorries proceeded to YPRES with section of 3rd Field Squadron R.E. 120 Grenades Hand and 120 Grenades Hand issued equally to 6th, 7th & 8th Brigades. Letter A.D. of S.M.T. rec'd. Subject: Provisional War establishment. Instruction therein complied with.	Ent
" 3rd	2 lorries returned from YPRES. Advance Section of 2 lorries with Ammunition proceeded to a billet on the POPERINGHE – OUDERDOM road. Lt E.H. Alldag in charge. 6 Trench Mortars with 96 bombs (95 mm) & necessary detonators, safety fuze, and Vesuvian matches issued to "K" Battery R.H.A. Eleven other ranks joined from N.C.N. Base.	Ent
" 4th	Coy routine only.	Ent

Army Form C. 2118.

WAR DIARY
INTELLIGENCE SUMMARY
(Erase heading not required.)

Instructions regarding War Diaries and Intelligence Summaries are contained in F. S. Regs, Part II. and the Staff Manual respectively. Title pages will be prepared in manuscript.

Hour, Date, Place	Summary of Events and Information	Remarks and references to Appendices
MORBECQUE 5.	One lorry sent to POPERINGHE with 1 x 3 grenades stand on rifle complete, 30 grenades rifle complete, 9 Bombs (95 m/m) and 98 Cartridges Signal Pistol "Very" bright Ball.	
"	Officer i/c advanced Section received instructions to remove derailed Staff Car from village of SILLIBECKE. Lorry despatched for this purpose, which joined Same to MORBECQUE for repairs to be carried out by 3rd Car Supply Column.	EHA
"	Coy Routine only.	EHA
7th	One lorry sent to Advanced Section with 88 grenade Rifle complete 75 " stand of rifle complete 102 " stand hydrolite and 235 Cartridges Signal "Very" bright B all.	EHA

WAR DIARY
INTELLIGENCE SUMMARY
(Erase heading not required.)

Army Form C. 2118.

Hour, Date, Place	Summary of Events and Information	Remarks and references to Appendices
MORBECQUE 7th Con.td	Orders rec'd from A.H. & Q.M.G. to draw from 2nd Car. Amm. Park, 9 grenades without detonators & some pistol "Very" light Ball. Cartridges. Order complied with.	SHA
" 8.15 "	3 Daimler lorries transferred to 116th Heavy Battery R.G.A. in exchange for 3 Albions. Daily duties only.	SHA
" 2 p.m. 9.15.	One lorry with ammunition despatched to Advanced Section. POPERINGHE-OUDERDON road. Wound there 4 p.m.	SHA
" 10.15	W. to H. Adday took over command of the park. from Major L.T. Savage. Advanced Section moved to St. JANS-TER-BIETEN.	SHA
	W. O. Campbell proceeded to Advanced Section with 8 additional lorries and food. Commenced. 4 Drivers transferred to 10 N.M.T. Depot for duty	SHA

Army Form C. 2118.

WAR DIARY
or
INTELLIGENCE SUMMARY
(Erase heading not required.)

Instructions regarding War Diaries and Intelligence Summaries are contained in F. S. Regs., Part II. and the Staff Manual respectively. Title pages will be prepared in manuscript.

Hour, Date, Place	Summary of Events and Information	Remarks and references to Appendices
MORBECQUE 11ᵗʰ	Recᵈ orders from A.A. & Q.M.G. 3ʳᵈ Corps to send 5 lorries to go to VIEUX-BERQUIN to pick up 400,000 rds. S.A.A. from 2ⁿᵈ Cav. Amm. Park. 200,000 rds. S.A.A. issued to IV Brigade Amm. Column at WALLON-CAPPEL. 2 Stafford lorries transferred to 8ᵗʰ Siege Battery R.G.A. in exchange for 2 Albions. D. of T. letter No 3037 received; Subject:- Provisional War Establishment, and revised A.F. B 213ᵇ. Notice for future guidance. Appointed 1 Sgt. 2 Corporals and 5 L/Corporals to complete establishment.	[signature]
12.15	Lorry sent to ST OMER for clothing and M.T. parts. Another to AIRE for wood to build up lorry bodies.	[signature]

Army Form C. 2118.

WAR DIARY
OF
INTELLIGENCE SUMMARY
(Erase heading not required.)

Instructions regarding War Diaries and Intelligence Summaries are contained in F. S. Regs., Part II. and the Staff Manual respectively. Title pages will be prepared in manuscript.

Hour, Date, Place	Summary of Events and Information	Remarks and references to Appendices
MORBECQUE 12th '15	Instructions received from AA & QMG to send an Officer and one lorry to YPRES, and report to him there at 5 P.m. Lt. A.P. WILLIAMS. proceeded, at 2-30 P.m & returned at 1 a.m. 13.2.15. Rec'd from II Cav. Div. Amm Col. at St JANS-TER-BIEXEN. 2,475 rds. S.A.A. Issued to XV Bde. Amm. Column at WALLON CAPPEL, 80,000 rds S.A.A.	S&A
" 2 P.m. 13th	At lorries sent to YPRES. At E.H. ALLDAY in charge. Returned 12 mid. night.	S&A
" 14th	Issued assortment of demolition to Royal Horse guards.	S&A
" 15th	One lorry with Ammunition sent to 3rd Cav. Amm Col. at WALLON CAPPEL. Another to O.i.c. O.M.F.R. for Spare M.T. parts	S&A

1247 W 3299 200,000 (E) 8/14 J.B.C.&A. Forms/C. 2118/11.

Army Form C. 2118.

WAR DIARY
INTELLIGENCE SUMMARY
(Erase heading not required.)

Instructions regarding War Diaries and Intelligence Summaries are contained in F. S. Regs., Part II. and the Staff Manual respectively. Title pages will be prepared in manuscript.

Hour, Date, Place	Summary of Events and Information	Remarks and references to Appendices
MORBECQUE 16/15	3 lorries containing 113,000 rds S.A.A. despatched to Amm. Column at WALLON CAPPEL; unloaded & proceeded to ARQUES to re load.	
	1 lorry sent to ARQUES and ST OMER for M.T. Parts.	EHA
3 P.m. "	N° 8 Lear, Field Ambulance received for repairs	
" 5 "	Completed.	
" 17/15	2 lorries containing 132,000 rds S.A.A sent to Amm Column at WALLON CAPPEL	
	At A.P.WILLIAMS proceeded to ST. OMER with two 30 cwt. Albions and exchanged same for two 3 ton Albions.	
	One 10 Cft and 3 men loaned from Army Troops Supply Column	EHA

Army Form C. 2118.

WAR DIARY
INTELLIGENCE SUMMARY
(Erase heading not required.)

Instructions regarding War Diaries and Intelligence Summaries are contained in F. S. Regs., Part II. and the Staff Manual respectively. Title pages will be prepared in manuscript.

Hour, Date, Place	Summary of Events and Information	Remarks and references to Appendices
MORBECQUE 17th cont.d	Women transferred to Army Troops Supply Column D. of S.T. letter No. 3133 rec.d Subject: Difficulty in obtaining lamps from ENGLAND. Instructions issued for all damaged lamps to be returned to Base for repairs.	
18th	Letter rec.d from A.P. of S.&T. 2nd.w Corps, Subject:- Weekly State of M.T. Vehicles and Return of Personnel and Vehicles, not required in future. Orders rec.d for One Officer with three lorries to report to 3rd Field Sqdn. R.E. for the purpose of proceeding to YPRES at 12.30 P.M. Three lorries despatched, W.O.O. CAMPBELL in charge.	End S.&T.
19th	58,000 rds S.A.A. issued to North Somerset Yeomanry and 160,000 rds to EV Bde. Amm. Column.	S.&T.

Army Form C. 2118.

WAR DIARY
or
INTELLIGENCE SUMMARY

(Erase heading not required.)

Instructions regarding War Diaries and Intelligence Summaries are contained in F. S. Regs., Part II. and the Staff Manual respectively. Title pages will be prepared in manuscript.

Hour, Date, Place	Summary of Events and Information	Remarks and references to Appendices
MORBECQUE 25.15	D. of T. circular memorandum No 78 recd Subject: Improved turnbuckles & links for Crawley-Boevey Non-Skids. 14 Demanded from advanced M.T. Depot	
10am "	One lorry with picks & shovels sent to a point West of LA BELLE HOTESSE, returned 4 pm	yes.
26.10	One lorry sent to LA BELLE HOTESSE with picks and shovels	
	One Sgt & One Private transferred to BASE Hospital	yes.
27.12	Lorry with picks & shovels sent to LA BELLE HOTESSE.	yes.
28.16	Lorry with shovels & picks sent to LA BELLE HOTESSE	yes.
"	3 men appointed to Corporals	yes.

Army Form C. 2118.

WAR DIARY
or
INTELLIGENCE SUMMARY

(Erase heading not required.)

Instructions regarding War Diaries and Intelligence Summaries are contained in F. S. Regs., Part II. and the Staff Manual respectively. Title pages will be prepared in manuscript.

Hour, Date, Place	Summary of Events and Information	Remarks and references to Appendices
MERBECQUE - General.	Total Ammunition issued during month: S.A.A 962,950 rds, Pistol Webley Ammn. 9828 rds, grenades Hand 774, grenades Rifle 239, Pistol "Very" Signal highball Cartridges 762, Bombs (95mm) 2,110. Trench mortars 1. Gunpowder for use with French mortars, 2.5 lbs. Also assortment of Demolition issued to Can. Regts. 78% of the coy and 33½% of R.F.A attached, inoculated during the month.	[signature]

Confidential

War Diary
of
3rd Cavalry Ammunition Park

From March 1st 1915 to March 31st 1915.

(Volume 2.)

Nil.

Army Form C. 2118.

WAR DIARY
of
INTELLIGENCE SUMMARY
(Erase heading not required.)

Instructions regarding War Diaries and Intelligence Summaries are contained in F. S. Regs., Part II. and the Staff Manual respectively. Title pages will be prepared in manuscript.

Hour, Date, Place	Summary of Events and Information	Remarks and references to Appendices
1st March 1915 MORBECQUE	One lorry with picks and shovels proceeded to LABELLE HOTESSE for the purpose of supplying tools for trench digging. Circular Memorandum from G.H.Q. on Transport M.T.1. Special permits issued for officers and others travelling in or through the area of any Allied Army.	Ref. ref. A.F2B.Rouen 5ª Issued with G.R.O. N.º 692. Div. R.O. 247.
2nd " "	One lorry with picks and shovels to LABELLE HOTESSE.	

WAR DIARY
INTELLIGENCE SUMMARY
(Erase heading not required.)

Army Form C. 2118.

Hour, Date, Place	Summary of Events and Information	Remarks and references to Appendices
3rd March 1915 MORBECQUE	One lorry with picks and shovels to LABELLE HOTESSE. Wire to ADMS for information as to notifying units of men transferred from Clearing Hospital to Base. Reply stating that men not discharged to unit in seven days are sent to Base. Governors on MT vehicles not the standard with: necessary action taken	D.A.T No. 2629/36. CJM.
4 " " 9.15 AM	One lorry with picks & shovels to LABELLE HOTESSE. Two lorries to FLETRE to pick up machine gun section of 2nd D.G's and took groomery out to convey them to their respective billets at BLARINGHEM and BOESEGHEM. Trials given with a view to minimising glare of kit. Report sent to OC CRE	CJM.

Army Form C. 2118.

WAR DIARY
of
INTELLIGENCE SUMMARY
(Erase heading not required.)

Instructions regarding War Diaries and Intelligence Summaries are contained in F. S. Regs., Part II. and the Staff Manual respectively. Title pages will be prepared in manuscript.

Hour, Date, Place	Summary of Events and Information	Remarks and references to Appendices
4th March 1915 MORBECQUE	Contents of scheme R.O. by G.O.C. II Army put on on thus knows	A & QMG 1/752
	Guns not to be stripped before return to base	S.R.O. 261 CJM
5th March 1915 9.15 AM	One lorry with picks and shovels to LABELLE HOTESSE. Arrived 11.15 AM	
2 PM " "	More second journey. Returned.	A & QMG 1/152
	Trials for transference of C.M. NoCa.	
	Extract from AD of S&T CC letter No 121/15 re Corps Rcy. NoCa.	AQC 110 S/D CJM
6 " "	Two lorries with picks and shovels to LABELLE HOTESSE. two journeys made.	
	Circular from GHQ re Presence of Officers. NoCa.	CJM

Army Form C. 2118.

WAR DIARY
INTELLIGENCE SUMMARY
(Erase heading not required.)

Hour, Date, Place	Summary of Events and Information	Remarks and references to Appendices
9th April 1916 MORBECQUE	The train did not arrive here until [illegible] here till the journey. Another Advance (Army School) of 3 [illegible] Other Advisors await for their report.	
	An Army [illegible] did not arrive anywhere near the journey. One Warfare Lorry went from Railway Station [illegible] for orders.	
	Attempt was of Carnet arising in person.	Sept '68
	List of nominations of [illegible] of officers of this sector.	Doc 107 Ab.

WAR DIARY
or
INTELLIGENCE SUMMARY.
(Erase heading not required.)

Army Form C. 2118.

Hour, Date, Place	Summary of Events and Information	Remarks and references to Appendices
9th March 1915 MORBECQUE	One lorry with kits and shovels to STAZEELE HOTESSE. Two journeys made. Orders received from A&QMG to distribute 438 shovels & 225 picks to various units on morning of 10th inst.	GM
10th March 1915	Shovels & picks distributed as above. Receipts received.	GM
11th March 1915	2nd Lieut. Amli: (Sydney Herbert) completed and returned. GOC's Order re Issue of Pay received varied Special Acquittance rolls to be kept for reference for two months. 64,000 Rounds S.A.A. to Ammunition train STRAZEELE.	99/J.180/697. S.A.O. 207 GM

Army Form C. 2118.

WAR DIARY
or
INTELLIGENCE SUMMARY.
(Erase heading not required.)

Instructions regarding War Diaries and Intelligence Summaries are contained in F.S. Regs., Part II. and the Staff Manual respectively. Title pages will be prepared in manuscript.

Hour, Date, Place	Summary of Events and Information	Remarks and references to Appendices
12th March 1915 HORBOQUE	Halford Lorry (Sanitary Section) completed stationed. Parts & Ambt: (Bior) arrived & have new springs fitted.	
	Memo: answer from O.C. Amb. 3rd Cav. Div. Calling attention to O.C. R.O. 183. Part Control: Noted	G.M.
13th "	Parts & Ambulance (Bior) completed and returned home.	
	Copy O's re: Regimental Rolls. Noted	A.F.T. 193/706.
	Officer detailed for the night on any station on M/C to report to Local Commander's Office. Noted	A.R.O. 2795 G.M.

WAR DIARY
or
INTELLIGENCE SUMMARY.
(Erase heading not required.)

Army Form C. 2118.

Hour, Date, Place	Summary of Events and Information	Remarks and references to Appendices
14th March 1915 MORBECQUE	1 NCO & 2 men returned previous establishment having been lost. Occupation of farm by troops noted.	OC 1091. CJM.
15th "	Four drivers joined from ROUEN. Return of all M.T. Vehicles in unit to be forwarded DBO. 306. to OC AVC on 20th Inst: Nominal roll of personnel serving in the unit sent.	DBO. 306. 20/T. 168. CJM.

Army Form C. 2118.

WAR DIARY
or
INTELLIGENCE SUMMARY.
(Erase heading not required.)

Instructions regarding War Diaries and Intelligence
Summaries are contained in F. S. Regs., Part II.
and the Staff Manual respectively. Title pages
will be prepared in manuscript.

Hour, Date, Place	Summary of Events and Information	Remarks and references to Appendices
16th March 1915. MORBECQUE	2 case of car being damaged report to be sent to O.C.A.S.C. NoGa	C.R.O. 497 & 36.
	Approval for issue of one chair and one pickaxe to every motor lorry. Also for 400 x 3" Cor adge Manilla Sewres to each Ammunition Park. 2 new cars.	Q.R.O. 316.
	Orders re discipline NoGa. troops to be in billets by 8.30 p.m. AM PM 6-8 pm. Cafés open 11-1 & 6-8 pm.	D.R.O. 318. GJM
17.	Sources re Country reports, reinforcements re-issued with G.R.O. No. 729. NoGa. Applications for personnel to be sent to G.H.Q. 3rd Echelon	G.R.O. 729. GJM

Army Form C. 2118.

WAR DIARY
or
INTELLIGENCE SUMMARY.
(Erase heading not required.)

Instructions regarding War Diaries and Intelligence Summaries are contained in F.S. Regs., Part II. and the Staff Manual respectively. Title pages will be prepared in manuscript.

Hour, Date, Place	Summary of Events and Information	Remarks and references to Appendices
17th March 1915 MODBECQUE	Aeroplanes notify fired on except by Boran of an officer of Machine Corps can be seen. Official time to be taken from Sir. Signal office. Nota.	G.R.O. 322. G.R.O. 323. Gen
18th March 1915	i 2t. Sucs RFA joined from 2nd Cav. Amm. Park. ii Nil report rendered re: interpreters who have rendered distinguished or valuable service. repeat iii Nil report rendered of Kitchens. iv 376 nds Pistol Webley Amm to North Som Yeo RHG 2nd L.G. Cav arts HQrs	i/CC. D5 AG B/134/207 i/CC. 1115 AG GHQ A/1697. O.f.k

WAR DIARY
or
INTELLIGENCE SUMMARY.
(Erase heading not required.)

Army Form C. 2118.

Hour, Date, Place	Summary of Events and Information	Remarks and references to Appendices
18th March 1915	136 Remain 13 Mar to IV th Bde: Amm: Col.	Cym
19th " " MORBECQUE	2/Lt R Balcarte - from RFA joint we now transfered to H.Qr RHA 3rd Cav: Div; ADy O.L.T letter recieved re 50% spare MT drivers. Demanded Provisional appointments noted	ADyST 239/1935 Q O/T 306 Cym
20th " "	553 Pistol Webley Amm. to 2nd G's " " " N.S. Yeomanry 276 " " " 3rd Cav Bn Signal Office 14904 " " " RHA Amm: Col.	Cym

Army Form C. 2118.

WAR DIARY
or
INTELLIGENCE SUMMARY.
(Erase heading not required.)

Instructions regarding War Diaries and Intelligence Summaries are contained in F.S. Regs., Part II. and the Staff Manual respectively. Title pages will be prepared in manuscript.

Hour, Date, Place	Summary of Events and Information	Remarks and references to Appendices
21st March 1915 Morbecque	M.T. Stores for Ammn. Parks in future conveyed to Supply Railhead	DQT 34 89
	Revised instructions re Casualty Reports & Reinforcement	8 R.O. 328 noted.
	3000 Rounds SAA moved to H/Q Cav. Corps 3000 " " " received from Railhead	Cfm
22nd March 1915 Morbecque	One lorry with préts kitchens proceeded to 6 Bde STEENBECQUE 7 " STAPLE 8 " EBBLINGHEM.	Cfm

Army Form C. 2118.

WAR DIARY
or
INTELLIGENCE SUMMARY.
(Erase heading not required.)

Instructions regarding War Diaries and Intelligence Summaries are contained in F. S. Regs., Part II. and the Staff Manual respectively. Title pages will be prepared in manuscript.

Hour, Date, Place	Summary of Events and Information	Remarks and references to Appendices
23rd March 1915 M. & R. B. & C. 90E.	Advance section D.A. & train continuing 1120 nds of 13th ammunition procession under 19th Coy R.E. to BAILLEUL. Ammunition taken over by 2nd Div. Amm. Park 538 Rounds Pistol H Colt Amm. issued to S.C. Car Bde. A.Q.	
24 " "	List of "Equipment" considered necessary for HQ of S.+ T. 252/15- a. w. to Army received. 5552 Rounds Pistol Webley Amm issued to 3rd Cav. H.Q. Q.R.C. Amm'd Retn issued of 6 Rounds 13/r to t. Amm : Col:	Cfm

Army Form C. 2118.

WAR DIARY
or
INTELLIGENCE SUMMARY.
(Erase heading not required.)

Instructions regarding War Diaries and Intelligence Summaries are contained in F.S. Regs., Part II. and the Staff Manual respectively. Title pages will be prepared in manuscript.

Hour, Date, Place	Summary of Events and Information	Remarks and references to Appendices
25th March 1915. MORBECQUE	1 Sgt & Corporal & 1/Cpl. appointed to Complete Establishment	
	The Lorry traversed Section did 56 rounds 13 Hrs. Returned empty	
	R.N. Section received 20 rounds 13 hrs from 2nd Div. St Omer Park.	CJM
	Orders re Regimentry & Purchasing received. Alter of ratios to be issued by 91 S.	DRO 344 WGA
	K of C	
	Base Stationary Depot formed at BOULOGNE	DRO 345.
26 " "	Remarks re Carbo Routine Order 166 dealing with office reinforcements. Also forth information in Para 4. C.C. 816 & A.G.G.H.Q. A/2270	NoGA DRO 348
	Orders re Sanitation of Billets received	NoGA DRO 348

WAR DIARY
or
INTELLIGENCE SUMMARY.
(Erase heading not required.)

Army Form C. 2118.

Hour, Date, Place	Summary of Events and Information	Remarks and references to Appendices
26th March 1915" MORBECQUE	Sent forward 60 men of HAZEBROUCK for baths. 50 Boxes & 3 for 95" Trench Mortars received 50 Detonators " " " 18 Forces Various details	JM
27 "	20 Flare pins Drivers dispatched from 11 Cluses ℬ Base in conference with Adjet Seller. Lt. Keiver Racing Captain Lindes in HAZEBROUCK out of bounds 1504 Pioneers Ammunition issued to RHG Par meet with issued 132 rounds 13 pdr to Amm. Col. 12 Boxes Various details to 3rd Dys	KD 1547 239 GRO 357 JM

Army Form C. 2118.

WAR DIARY
or
INTELLIGENCE SUMMARY.
(Erase heading not required.)

Instructions regarding War Diaries and Intelligence Summaries are contained in F.S. Regs., Part II. and the Staff Manual respectively. Title pages will be prepared in manuscript.

Hour, Date, Place	Summary of Events and Information	Remarks and references to Appendices
28th March 1915 MORBEO QUE	One lorry to Adv. Section with petrol. General instructions from G.H.Q. re: transfer of units from one formation to another. Definition of "Formation" A Command which is in direct communication with G.H.Q. Issued 50 Bombs) J. Gifford to 50 Detonators) Verdun 3rd Field Tps R.E. 6 Boxes Verinia bullets 6 PHR. Adv. Section received 136 rounds 13 lbs from 2nd Div Ammn. Park.	[signature]

Army Form C. 2118.

WAR DIARY
or
INTELLIGENCE SUMMARY
(Erase heading not required.)

Hour, Date, Place	Summary of Events and Information	Remarks and references to Appendices
29th March 1915 MORBECQUE	Every train below will return	GRO 353
	Letter re Courts Martial concerning trying a soldier	" 356
	charged with an offence whilst on duty as such	" 357
	Straw for use in limber Saucepan	
	Issued 5000 RPA to RHG's 1504 Pistols ready to 3rd DG 10 horses ready to 2nd GL's	
	Return from 5000 STA. 1504 Wily Pistol 10 horses returned	
	Our Action moved 124 mes 13th to Henin Al. Instructions for remounting outlying armies unit GRO No 684. Across the belt was in monthly	Jan

WAR DIARY
or
INTELLIGENCE SUMMARY
(Erase heading not required.)

Army Form C. 2118.

Hour, Date, Place	Summary of Events and Information	Remarks and references to Appendices
30th March 1915 MORBECQUE	Lorry driven Section with rations. Received from Railhead 6 boxes matches (M.V.). Am. Section received 36 rounds 13 hr. from 2nd Div. Amm. Park.	CJM
31st March 1915 "	Lorry driven Section with rations. Am. Section received 36 rounds 13 hr. from 2nd Am. Park.	CJM CJM Major OC 3rd Cav Bde Amm 1 Park

121/5204

Confidential.

War Diary
of
3rd Cavalry Ammunition Park.

From 1st April 1915   To 30th April 1915.

(Volume 5.)

Army Form C. 2118.

WAR DIARY
or
INTELLIGENCE SUMMARY.
(Erase heading not required.)

Place	Date	Hour	Summary of Events and Information	Remarks and references to Appendices
MORBECQUE	1/30 April		Lorry to advanced section at BAILLEUL with rations.	
			Advanced section issued 128 rounds 13 pdr	
			Repairs to Sunbeam M.T. 1812	
			Instructions issued that in future all casualties abroad be sent to S.A.G. 3rd Echelon	G/m.
			Received 62 horses Russian metals from railhead	
	2"		Lorry to advanced section with rations	
			H.G. action No 6 under repair	
			Sunbeam Ambulance M.T. 1114 in for repair	
			Boots to repair 1870 to O.C. PARIS	GRO 365
			Discipline effect of vehicles received spoiled on board	" 364 G/m
			No officer or man except on duty will visit the area occupied by the French or Belgian Armies without authority from GHQ	GRO 434 G/m

Army Form C. 2118.

WAR DIARY
or
INTELLIGENCE SUMMARY.
(Erase heading not required.)

Instructions regarding War Diaries and Intelligence Summaries are contained in F. S. Regs., Part II. and the Staff Manual respectively. Title pages will be prepared in manuscript.

Place	Date	Hour	Summary of Events and Information	Remarks and references to Appendices
MORBECQUE	3rd night		Lorry to advanced section with rations	
			Funken Ambulance 1114 & Albion HQ No 6 finished	
			Returns rendered direct to Col. I/C A.D.C. section & G's Office	A DS + S 306/15 gml.
			Should be sent by D.R.L.S.	
"	4th "		Lorry to advanced section with rations.	
			Advanced section issued 104 rounds 13 pdr	Gm.
			276 rounds Pistol Webley to A.V.C. & 5 Cav. Bde.	
"	6th "		Lorry to advanced section with rations	
			Albion No 10	
			Sunbeam 17 A 18·3 3 for repair	
			1000 rounds S.A.A. Outfitting to Railhead	
			100 " " 13 pdr " "	
			276 " " R.W. " R.H.G's	
			50 " " 95 Grand mortar to 3rd field squadron R.E.	Gm.

1577   Wt. W10791/1773   500,000   1/15   D. D. & L.   A.D.S.S./Form/C. 2118.

WAR DIARY
or
INTELLIGENCE SUMMARY.

(Erase heading not required.)

Army Form C. 2118.

Place	Date	Hour	Summary of Events and Information	Remarks and references to Appendices
MORBECQUE	April 5		G: 1098 cheques sent for deficiencies despatched to Ordnance. 50 Bombs .95 Mortars from STRAZEELE.	CJM
	" 6 "		Sorry to advance section. Letter received from AA & QMG concerning increased reserves that SAA to taken to increase the percentage given out. 6 Boxes Primers to 3rd S.G's 6 " Ne. Charges " " 6 Detonators " " No 8 Safety fuze 3 20 yds fuze instantaneous " 3 Coils " Safety No 8 "	AA & QMG 1/1095 CJM

Army Form C. 2118.

WAR DIARY
or
INTELLIGENCE SUMMARY.
(Erase heading not required.)

Place	Date	Hour	Summary of Events and Information	Remarks and references to Appendices
MORBECQUE	7th April		H.Q. No 9 under repair	
			Triumph Cycle No 7 "	Gm.
			Lorry advanced section with rations	
	8th "		Return sent to A.D.S.&T. stating our average consumption of Petrol & Lubricants on when motor lorries on the move	
			Left support to IV Th Div. Supply Col:	
			Return re Promotion of W.O's & N.C.O's received instal.	G20759
			Advanced section issued 120 rounds 13th .	
			" received 108 " "	
			Return called for showing numbers & types of fire extinguishers in use in the unit	ADQS+T 322/15
			Price list of clothing and equipment received	
			Instructions issued re Requisitioning & Billeting to be returned to A.D.R.S.	ADQS+T 331/15
			H.Q No 9 under repair	Gm.

Army Form C. 2118.

WAR DIARY
or
INTELLIGENCE SUMMARY.
(Erase heading not required.)

Place	Date	Hour	Summary of Events and Information	Remarks and references to Appendices
MORBECQUE	9th April		Lorry taken, motors with rations	appx
"	10 "	"	Bought green vegetables in Saint Omer.	appx.
"	11 "	"	Lorry to ambulance with rations.	
"	"	"	Lorry to advanced section with rations.	
"	"	"	BRO 378 Rects for Hydroscopes the forwarded to DADOS	appx
"	12 "	"	Crossley Ambulance 3438 for repair	
"	"	"	Lorry to advanced section	
"	"	"	Billeting in Schools to cease	970379
"	"	"	Office of OC claims Committee established in SAINT OMER	" 380
"	"	"	Return of officers + other ranks rendered to AA & QMG on 3rd of each month no longer required	" 381
"	"	"		appx

1577 Wt. W10791/1773 500,000 1/15 D. D. & L. A.D.S.S./Forms/C. 2118.

Army Form C. 2118.

WAR DIARY
or
INTELLIGENCE SUMMARY.
(Erase heading not required.)

Instructions regarding War Diaries and Intelligence Summaries are contained in F. S. Regs., Part II. and the Staff Manual respectively. Title pages will be prepared in manuscript.

Place	Date	Hour	Summary of Events and Information	Remarks and references to Appendices
MORBECQUE	13th April		Lorry to advanced station with rations Sunbeam Ambulance (Sydney Plunkett) for repair Douglas 5 H.P. lightcar overhauled.	JM
"	14 "	"	Lorry to advanced station with rations Transfer of vehicles noted Misuse of green envelope AF W 307 D. noted Crossley Ambulance finished Sunbeam 1812 finished 552 Rounds P.W. to 3rd D.G.s	ADS&T 354/15 CC 1311 JM
"	15 "	"	Lieut Allday to Indian Cavalry Corps to attend C.M. Lorry to advanced station with rations Doubled rebels tube sent to G.H.Q. Troops Supply Col. advanced section — issued 60 rounds 1812 " " " received 72 " "	D of S 3764 JM

1577 Wt.W10791/1773 500,000 1/15 D. D. & L. A.D.S.S./Form/C. 2118.

Army Form C. 2118.

WAR DIARY
or
INTELLIGENCE SUMMARY.
(Erase heading not required.)

Instructions regarding War Diaries and Intelligence Summaries are contained in F. S. Regs., Part II. and the Staff Manual respectively. Title pages will be prepared in manuscript.

Place	Date	Hour	Summary of Events and Information	Remarks and references to Appendices
MORBECQUE	April 16th		Lieut Allday proceeded to Cour Marles at HRE Albion Lorry No 9 Station to ISBERGUES for retyring. MT stores earlier the day to Base MT Depot Lorry park. Return nil return	DofT 376th C/fm.
"	17th		Lorry to an used delong will return Remants for reinforcements the renewed weekly. 67 Men on taking 820392 thirty Ammunition return to Base ammunition in park of Residence at 12 Noon on Sunday. Billeting returns to be renewed weekly. Original to go on Duplicate to O i/c Branch Requisition Office Triplicate to be retained	[signature]

Army Form C. 2118.

WAR DIARY
or
INTELLIGENCE SUMMARY.
(Erase heading not required.)

Place	Date	Hour	Summary of Events and Information	Remarks and references to Appendices
MORBECQUE	18th Cap		Lorry Advanced section will return	
			Advanced section visited to Ammunition Col. 104 Rounds 13 plr	
			36 Rounds 13 plr	820 395
			received from Railhead	
			Branch requisition Office established at 25 Rue D'Aire HAZEBROUCK	
			Officer going to PARIS to report on arrival to the APM 3, Boulevard des Invalides	CJM
"	19"		Lorry to Adv. Section with rations	820 397
			Pow. Cars only to be used on duty	
			Recd 5 copies of extracts from G.R.O.	AA.QMG/99
			Halford Lorry WD 3259 Sanitary Section No 12 for repair	CJM
"	20"		Lorry to adv. Section with rations	
			Drafts of reinforcements to be kept referred for a period of 14 days	820 399
			When rendering AFB 213A it is to be stated whether surpluses or deficiency of WO's are Class 1 or Class 2	CJM

Army Form C. 2118.

WAR DIARY
or
INTELLIGENCE SUMMARY.
(Erase heading not required.)

Place	Date	Hour	Summary of Events and Information	Remarks and references to Appendices
MORBECQUE	April 21		Ruling white allowance of fuel for cooking purposes laid down in A.R. 947 or Equivalents in G.R.O. 374 is sufficient. Answered in affirmative.	QMG 79½
			Grant of £3 for Officers & Sergts horses two not able to take force	Sgt 394
			When necessary Divisn Forges may be used	GRO 781
			Requisitions for coal to be sent in 24 hrs in advance	GRO 400
			Issues of Ammunition 7000 rounds .303 to N.S.Y. Comany 552 " P.W. 13 Boxes V. matches " 10 " " P.D. 9's 7000 rounds .303 " 552 " P.W.	
			Receipts 72 Boxes V matches from STRAZEELE	
			Indian 1512 for retain owing to accumn. Brought in to Army HQ No 6	
			Indian 1113 No 6 Field Amb. lubried & finished M 1110 8 " " retd for retain	ofin

Army Form C. 2118.

WAR DIARY
or
INTELLIGENCE SUMMARY.
(Erase heading not required.)

Instructions regarding War Diaries and Intelligence Summaries are contained in F. S. Regs., Part II. and the Staff Manual respectively. Title pages will be prepared in manuscript.

Place	Date	Hour	Summary of Events and Information	Remarks and references to Appendices
MORBECQUE	April 22		Lorry to advanced section with rations. Ammunition receipts 7000 Rounds 303 from R Head STRAZEELE 652 " " " PW	
"	23		Workshops HQ Lorry No 2 overhauled Ambulance M 1110 8th Field Amb. finished received Workshops Lorry Body for Ambulance 3rd Car. finished Ambulance Amb. M 1112 Entered Workshop Gunner Car despatched Base: Return after completion of repair.	
"	24		Lorry to adv. section with rations Ammunition Rounds No. 5 6 7. of 2nd Batt. to RENINGHELST Ditto 200,000 S.A.A Entered 6 Amm: Col Receipts 200,000 SAA from Railhead.	

1577 Wt. W10791/1773 500,000 1/15 D. D. & L. A.D.S.S./Form/C. 2118.

Army Form C. 2118.

WAR DIARY
or
INTELLIGENCE SUMMARY.
(Erase heading not required.)

Instructions regarding War Diaries and Intelligence Summaries are contained in F. S. Regs., Part II. and the Staff Manual respectively. Title pages will be prepared in manuscript.

Place	Date	Hour	Summary of Events and Information	Remarks and references to Appendices
MORBECQUE	April 25		Lorry G.S.W. Nelson with petrol.	
			Ammunition Issues by A.A.C. Det. 75th rounds 13 pr. } from Railhead	Gm.
			receipts " " 18 pr. "	
			Motor Bicycle N° 6 to GHQ Troops Supp Col. Forestier. 2 went on Base ROUEN for new motor cycle	
			Lorry G.S.W. Nelson with rations	
			Ammunition Issues 120 rounds very Pist. to RHG's } from Railhead	
	26		Receipts 120 " " "	
			5000 " .303 SAA "	
			Workshops Mercedes Amb: of Cav: Bde. finished	
			Correspondence Received in further list of issues of supplies in the Departments Du Nord + Pas de Calais	Gm.

Army Form C. 2118.

WAR DIARY
or
INTELLIGENCE SUMMARY.

(Erase heading not required.)

Place	Date	Hour	Summary of Events and Information	Remarks and references to Appendices
MORBECQUE	April 27		Lorry park; kits with ration	
			Correspondence. When running parts for motor cycles they are freely stored to store.	2 off 30671
			A certificate to be sent showing that there is no surplus of motor cycles	GRO 800
			Rec'd. pamphlet of instruction re Army (Inspection of Ordnance) Act	GRO EFA
	28		Distinguishing marks put on 13 New vehicles	
			Lorry park; section with ration	
			Workshop: No. 6 Section 2 for repair.	
			Correspondence. Supplies to be handed in to Senior Ordnance or Transport Officer DRO 401
			A record is also to be kept by units from Griffin of which motor	
			ammunition.	AAQMG 8/367 EFA
			2 cases of recovery ammunition may be drawn from ABEELE	

1577 Wt. W10791/1773 500,000 1/15 D. D. & L. A.D.S.S./Forms/C. 2118.

Army Form C. 2118.

WAR DIARY
or
INTELLIGENCE SUMMARY.
(Erase heading not required.)

Instructions regarding War Diaries and Intelligence Summaries are contained in F. S. Regs., Part II. and the Staff Manual respectively. Title pages will be prepared in manuscript.

Place	Date	Hour	Summary of Events and Information	Remarks and references to Appendices
HORBECQUE	Apl 29		Lorry barr. her will return	
			Inspected by Major Coulson A.S.C.	
			It away to No2 Motor Amb. Convoy	
			" Williams taken over No2 section	
			2 Lt Campbell taken over No1 section	
			Motorlists No6 list 2 for repair	Ofm
"	30		Lorry barr. section with rations	
			Ammunition issue 96 rounds 13 pdr 6 a.m.bat.	
			receipt 96 " " "	
			" " from Railhead	
			Motorlists Daimler lorry No 6 section 2) to retain	
			Albion " " " 9 1 3)	Ofm

C. J. Martin Capt A.S.C.
OC 3rd Cav Amm Park.

137/5526

3rd Cavalry Division

Confidential

War Diary
of
3rd Cav Ammn. Park.

From 1st May 1915.   to 31st May 1915.

(Volume II)

Army Form C. 2118.

WAR DIARY
or
INTELLIGENCE SUMMARY.
(Erase heading not required.)

Instructions regarding War Diaries and Intelligence Summaries are contained in F. S. Regs., Part II. and the Staff Manual respectively. Title pages will be prepared in manuscript.

Place	Date	Hour	Summary of Events and Information	Remarks and references to Appendices
MORBECQUE	May 1st		Lorry Ambulance section Banguer (will return)	GRO 820 C/o
			Doses of fuel for Morning Purposes Drawn	
	2		Lorry Ambulance section will return	
			Return on inspection received from Major Leybourne Smith with regard to:—	
			1. Lubrications	
			2. Periodical inspection of motor ambulances	
			Note cars only to be driven by ASC drivers allotted to them	GRO 808
			Precautions in case of fire	GRO 810 C/o
			Ambulance Convoy to 1115 in for plan	
	3		Lorry Ambulance Section will return	
			Pte Wilson } to 1st Cav Div Sup Col:	
			Pte Menton } 15 rations	

1577 Wt. W10791/1773 500,000 1/15 D. D. & L.   A.D.S.S./Forms/C. 2118.

Army Form C. 2118.

WAR DIARY
or
INTELLIGENCE SUMMARY.
(Erase heading not required.)

Instructions regarding War Diaries and Intelligence Summaries are contained in F. S. Regs., Part II. and the Staff Manual respectively. Title pages will be prepared in manuscript.

Place	Date	Hour	Summary of Events and Information	Remarks and references to Appendices
MORBECQUE	May 2nd		Sergt Stone posted from 1st San Bur KC	ADS & Y x 2/142
			Pte Hawley " Boa MT Dept ROUEN	
			Motor Ambulance Cars for repair to be sent GHQ troops MC	ADS & Y 238/15
			Pte G. Hall 175/1088 transferred BMT Dept ROUEN	
			Cars Numbers ADC'd Cars number censor letters number also	Dy 3 441/15
			Posted in all correspondence	
			Bus raised by M T Vehicles away Indent files leaving on the	
			Ground Carload files to be added.	A.M.O.M.C 261/15
			Received memorandum from Ca. Cars attached HQ L 3rd W 3104. &c	
			Tauplier Army (Registration of Cauteens) Act	J.U.
			Odo. section received approved 132 rounds B.L.W.	

Army Form C. 2118.

WAR DIARY
or
INTELLIGENCE SUMMARY.
(Erase heading not required.)

Place	Date	Hour	Summary of Events and Information	Remarks and references to Appendices
MORBECQUE	May 4	5. 6. 8. 10 1. 2. 3 L	No 1 Section Barnard Baton from advanced station. When requisitioning cars to be known for which the Car is required must be stated. M1114 8th Field Amb. is for repair	920414
			Army Advanced Section not rationed A.B. 64 B.C. checked for mistakes Triumph Motor cycle attached to 8th Field Ambulance) in for repair Sunbeam 4th Field Ambulance H.Q. No 2. Daimler M184. Section No 6.	20.3975

Army Form C. 2118.

WAR DIARY
or
INTELLIGENCE SUMMARY.
(Erase heading not required.)

Place	Date	Hour	Summary of Events and Information	Remarks and references to Appendices
MORBECQUE	May 6th		Army armoured section sick return	ADS of J 6/5/15
			MSc Ambulances with the Division the inspected monthly by the 3rd Can Amm Park	
			PO Melbourn for duty to Amm Park from No. 2 MT Base ROUEN. SS Woodner joker RHA from No. 2 General Base HAVRE	Jm
			Number Mob Amb. 1115 A Echelon for repair Number 2 No. 6 Damlis to repair	
		7	Not 2 No 3 branchel election and ratros Alkin Army Res.1 No 4 } to repair " 6 }	Jm
			Number Amb M 1111 B Echelon for repair	

Army Form C. 2118.

WAR DIARY
or
INTELLIGENCE SUMMARY.
(Erase heading not required.)

Instructions regarding War Diaries and Intelligence Summaries are contained in F. S. Regs., Part II. and the Staff Manual respectively. Title pages will be prepared in manuscript.

Place	Date	Hour	Summary of Events and Information	Remarks and references to Appendices
MORBECQUE	May 8/7		Return HALO lorry to adv; section with material	Adj J Memorandum No. 83
			Inversion of Gamble lorries. This will only take over for stores & shackle bolts.	
			Sick wastage return to be made up & Friday 6 PM & showed the forwarded hence to ADMS office no later than 5 PM on Saturday.	GRO 421
			IAA the collector handed over to Railhead Commandant for return to Ordnance at the Base.	GRO 420
			Rev: below round reserve 116 Rounds 13 Pdr.	AJH

1577 Wt.W10791/1773 500,000 1/15 D. D. & L. A.D.S.S./Forms/C. 2118.

Army Form C. 2118.

WAR DIARY
or
INTELLIGENCE SUMMARY.
(Erase heading not required.)

Place	Date	Hour	Summary of Events and Information	Remarks and references to Appendices
MORBECQUE	May 9th		No 5 2nd Section advanced section not retd	
			R.C. officers invited to H.Q. as we have an officer's mess	
			opened off the chapel	
			Pte Minnock who had joined from ROUEN	
			No letter staff reporting to GRO 709 Bks of officers leaves GHQ 2 21/7/43	
			wounded in No CO	
			Return of wheels to be sent in to Col i/c Amb Section AGS/ffs 8045 3ms	
			with Copy to Fh Field Amb received	CJM
"	"	10¹⁵	No 6 2nd Section took over section with retd	
			Sec 1 No 6 } sent for repair	
			Sec 3 No 6 }	
			Inspections started	
			From the round three weekly Idr 225 from	
			Hunceton from Chief of French Mission at Hazebrouck	

1577 Wt. W10791/1773 500,000 1/15 D. D. & L. A.D.S.S./Forms/C. 2118.

WAR DIARY
or
INTELLIGENCE SUMMARY.

Army Form C. 2118.

Place	Date	Hour	Summary of Events and Information	Remarks and references to Appendices
M7286-5946	May/9		Returns inoculation reqd weekly by ADMS from all units made up to 6 PM every Friday & in office of ADMS by 5 PM on Saturday. Weekly return of shortages when no sufficient notice given. Return of inoculation. Return of movement. ½ made to AB 6k.	DRO 426
			No 3 Sec 3rd. Sidi Bar will return Sec 1 No 1 ¾ 6 } for relief HQ 4 } 10 } for relief	GM
"	11		SAA the mentioned for Moto Machine gun section attached to 103 M6 3rd Car Sir Barir in General allowance to machine gun.	103 M6 1/1487 GM

WAR DIARY
or
INTELLIGENCE SUMMARY.

(Erase heading not required.)

Army Form C. 2118.

Place	Date	Hour	Summary of Events and Information	Remarks and references to Appendices
MORBECQUE	May 11		Received from 3rd Can A.C. Denham, Bell, Flack	Cu
			To 3rd/1 Supply Col. Bell, Slade, Davis	
			Received from Aviole Germany 6000 rounds 303	

WAR DIARY
or
INTELLIGENCE SUMMARY.

(Erase heading not required.)

Army Form C. 2118.

Instructions regarding War Diaries and Intelligence Summaries are contained in F. S. Regs., Part II. and the Staff Manual respectively. Title pages will be prepared in manuscript.

Place	Date	Hour	Summary of Events and Information	Remarks and references to Appendices
MORBECQUE	12		1st Rein. No 7 draw Lester will return "Winton" and Sydney Newbold to Field and for repair 2 Rein. No 6 " " " " for repair 1 " " " " " 3rd Can. Div. Joints Tenders SAA Section of Amm. Col. Lowacked 800x S.A.R in LEMMERTINGHE SAA Adv. Section of Amm. Park will skirmish from HQ attacked Lowacked to 1mm one mile SSW of P. in POPERINGHE on POPERINGHE–RENINGHELST road Remainder of No 1 Sec. 13 km of BAILLEUL Adv. Rertion issued received 120 rounds 13 pdr: 6000 SAA 200 Rounds 18pdr HE } from Railhead 100 Lbs Hard Powder } 50 Fuses No 80	Ref No 5 A Q/n

1557 Wt. W10791/1773 500,000 1/15 D.D. & L. A.D.S.S./Forms/C. 2118.

WAR DIARY
or
INTELLIGENCE SUMMARY.
(Erase heading not required.)

Army Form C. 2118.

Instructions regarding War Diaries and Intelligence Summaries are contained in F. S. Regs., Part II. and the Staff Manual respectively. Title pages will be prepared in manuscript.

Place	Date	Hour	Summary of Events and Information	Remarks and references to Appendices
MOZEECOOE	13		Lorry took sections with rations	20/12/15
			Damaged cars & lorries of French make placed in our care for repair	
			Ambulance returned Ypres	
			6401.000 BMC to 44th section Ann. Col.	Cm
			620.000 " " " from MBEELE	
"	14		Lorry NO.9 took section with rations. Remain attached to No.4 section.	ADG.sv.s 11/9/15
			Recd. 1 No 1 } to retain stores	
			No 7 }	
			New Fordin no.166 entered in AB 64	ADsvs
			MT vehicles sent to GHQ for repair ordered to complete with all	
			gear recently carried see Circular NO. 233/15 ADsvs	
			156 rounds 13/2 issued received	Cm
			6000 " 303 Dog Dg's	
			6000 Hotchkiss from 7th Div MBEELE	
			383	

1577 Wt. W10791/1773 500,000 1/15 D. D. & L. A.D.S.S./Forms/C. 2118.

WAR DIARY
INTELLIGENCE SUMMARY

Army Form C. 2118.

Place	Date	Hour	Summary of Events and Information	Remarks and references to Appendices
HORSEGGOE	15		Rev. Mahon inspected by DS Wilkinson & necessary repairs noted	
			HQ No 9 from SHA Advanced Relw	
			HQ No 10 Order taken out Action	8.R.o.430
			Reinforcement of Ration — rolls	
	16		Casualties in action will be shown on Sick Wastage Report	8.R.o.434
			Graves Registration Committee	CC4007 GRO 846
			Officers Allowances	"848
			RHA 6th 3CD Bde known as "RHD Bde"	
			Precautions to be taken to avoid leakage from vehicles running oil	9.7. Anicle Memorandum No. P3
			Rec. Chandler 1000 miles for lorry & one in two months. Daily cleaning outlined in Vehicle Book	
			2000 " Car "	
			HQ No 7 NOT meet } from Mahon	

Army Form C. 2118.

WAR DIARY
or
INTELLIGENCE SUMMARY.
(Erase heading not required.)

Instructions regarding War Diaries and Intelligence Summaries are contained in F. S. Regs., Part II. and the Staff Manual respectively. Title pages will be prepared in manuscript.

Place	Date	Hour	Summary of Events and Information	Remarks and references to Appendices
MORBECQUE	16		Sudan Amt. Sydney Kurkurt Issues 276 rounds P.W. 8793 Coy .303 5900 S.A.A. Sector Arm Park 5400	
	17		Recd. 1000 V.P. Flares from STRAZEELE H.Q. No 10 took Section Superintending on H.Q. No 8 Formation Section 8°2°a taken	
	18		H.Q. No 7 Adv: Rct Taken 1812 Painted Superintending to H.Q.k H.Q. No 6 Advanced Section H.Q. Repair & Manuval Sara Action Noted	MSKS aus/1/15

1577 Wt. W10791/1773 500,000 1/15 D. D. & L. A.D.S.S./Forms/C. 2118.

WAR DIARY
or
INTELLIGENCE SUMMARY.

Army Form C. 2118.

Place	Date	Hour	Summary of Events and Information	Remarks and references to Appendices
MORBECQUE	19		Return strength & also sent in to O/c Fricy Beach SSO & 974 Thursday.	SSO 298 3CD
			HQ No.10 to Supostrahes	
"	20		HQ No.10 to Mr. Retow	
			1200 rounds 13 dr transferred ON 01 Ammn.Park LILLERS	
			HQ No 7 Rylers initiales	
			3rd Cav. Into Lyall RWR Downers Car Motor for rehair	GJM
			HQ No 10 own Return.	
	21		Promotions Lieut Williams to Capt.	
			Davies " "	
			2/Lt Campbell to Lieut	
	22		HQ No 10 to own Motor with rations	GJM

WAR DIARY
or
INTELLIGENCE SUMMARY.
(Erase heading not required.)

Army Form C. 2118.

Place	Date	Hour	Summary of Events and Information	Remarks and references to Appendices
MORT CORE 23	23		HQ No 14 Base Return will return	
			Return of Ammunition in possession of units at 12 noon on Wednesday 26th to be sent Office of A.D.M.S.	GRo 863
			Innumerable motor cycles to be returned to Base Depot. The O.C. M.T. Base who will demand from OC adv M.T. depot any bicycle which may be required in replacement	GRo 857
			Regn. & form Encl. Ref. DADO Ret. 1893	GRo 4447
			H.Q. of Division moves to RENESCURE	F 104
	24		HQ No 7 Base Return O/C are section A.P.S. Office Base Attached on duty to be shown on strength of unit	9/4

WAR DIARY
or
INTELLIGENCE SUMMARY.

(Erase heading not required.)

Army Form C. 2118.

Place	Date	Hour	Summary of Events and Information	Remarks and references to Appendices
MCRBIGOVE	24		Res recent moved 100 Rounds 13dr D3rd Bn. Div Am. Col. 200 " " Anti aircraft Section 500 " " 1st Ca. Div A.P. No 13 La. Col. moved without reference to D.A.A. & Q.M.G. Ca. Div.	gm
"	25		M9 N0 8 Wk reboots draw Rations Note on Protection against Poisonous gases No 1 Section returned to Park at 6.20 pm. Coul. G. is now 13 lm available.	OA 2/180 A/30 gm

Army Form C. 2118.

WAR DIARY
or
INTELLIGENCE SUMMARY.
(Erase heading not required.)

Instructions regarding War Diaries and Intelligence Summaries are contained in F. S. Regs., Part II. and the Staff Manual respectively. Title pages will be prepared in manuscript.

Place	Date	Hour	Summary of Events and Information	Remarks and references to Appendices
MORBECQUE	May 26		Pte. MURDOCH & STAVELEY to Base; surplus.	
			M.S.M. G. BASS joined from G.H.Q. Troops Supply Column, surplus to est&c.	
			Wired Reinfs. Base for instructions re disposal.	
			No 13 pr. Amn available at Railhead.	
			Superstition Pct 2.1. Pct E. u. M.G.Cyle No. 3. Overhaul.	Que
			Issued. To Emu 47. 20,000 S.A.A.	
			764 Pistol Webley	
			S.A.A.	
			R.N.S.D. 2,000	
			552 Pistol Webley	
			40 Prismn	
			18 DeConlin	
	27		No 13 pr. ppt available at Railhead.	
			Issued. To Amn. Col. 53,000 S.A.A.	
			Maxstoch 5,000 "	
			R.N.S.D. 6 hours Ves. Watch	
			Capt. C.J. Martin, O.C. granted leave of absence from 27th to 30th.	Que

1577 Wt. W10791/1773 500,000 1/15 D. D. & L. A.D.S.S./Forms/C. 2118.

Army Form C. 2118.

WAR DIARY
or
INTELLIGENCE SUMMARY.
(Erase heading not required.)

Instructions regarding War Diaries and Intelligence Summaries are contained in F. S. Regs., Part II. and the Staff Manual respectively. Title pages will be prepared in manuscript.

Place	Date	Hour	Summary of Events and Information	Remarks and references to Appendices
MERBECQUE	May 28		No 13 pr. Ammn. not available. Receipts. Railhead (STRAZEELE) Issued. 4,000 rds S.A.A. to 1st Royal Dragoons. 69,000 S.A.A. 552 P.W. 48 Artillery 40 horses	O/u
	29		No 13 pr. not available. Issued. 10,000 rds. S.A.A. to Scots Greys. (29th) 360 Shells 60 H.E.Sh.1 30 " 2. Left Horses, motorcyclist attached to 4th Bn. R.N.D. N.B. Ars. used for horses.	
	30		Capt. C.J. Martin granted return of Amn. due 4th prox. No 13 pr. not available. Issued to S.A. Sub. Annulet (now VLAMERTINGHE) 175 Hand Grenades, smoke explosive 60 " " M.1 90 " " Short Rifle 600 Cartridges, Very Pistol	O/u

WAR DIARY
or
INTELLIGENCE SUMMARY.

(Erase heading not required.)

Army Form C. 2118.

Place	Date	Hour	Summary of Events and Information	Remarks and references to Appendices
MORBECQUE	May 31		13 pm, not yet arrived. Lieut. W.O. Campbell granted leave of absence till 3rd June. Issued to S.A.A. sect. Amm. Col. by lony EVLAMERTINGHE 6,000 rds S.A.A. Also received from railhead.	
	Jun 1		13 pm, not yet arrived. Issued to S.A.A. Amm. Col. by lorry EVLAMERTINGHE — Bombs for Trench Mortar, Hand Grenades No. 1 — 50, No. 5 — 24, Catridges V. Pistol — 240, Grenades No. 6 — 75. Received. Rain seems to ease from dust except under exceptional circumstances S.A.A. Establishment raised from 560,000 rds to 670,000 rds — owing to machine guns being attached to Bde. 2 men being to be demanded. Cyprination left sage Park. O.C. 3rd Cav Ammn	

3rd Cavalry Division.

121/5971.

Confidential

War Diary

of

3rd Car Ammn Park

From 1st June 1915 to 30th June 1915.

(Volume 5)

Army Form C. 2118.

WAR DIARY
or
INTELLIGENCE SUMMARY.
(Erase heading not required.)

Place	Date	Hour	Summary of Events and Information	Remarks and references to Appendices
MOROCCO	June 1		13th not yet available. Issued 57th Amm. Col. 4.84 Bombs for Trench Mortars 50 Lansgranate No 1. Received same from Ordnance 24 " " 5 240 Cartridges V Pist Col " " 75 Grenades No 6. " " Run line telegraphic not except under exceptional circumstances NAA Establishment raised from 580,000 rounds to 690,000 owing to extra machine guns having been attached to Divisions. This more tonnie necessary.	G.or

WAR DIARY
INTELLIGENCE SUMMARY

Place	Date	Hour	Summary of Events and Information	Remarks and references to Appendices
MORBECQUE	June 2		No 13 pr. gun arrived. No more 13 pr. to be drawn from Ord. Corps. Sanction for Col. Cmdt. com. to FLAMERTINGHE issued.	DDOS M.G. A.10511 2/6/15 [sig]
				Col. Cmdt. A.1058 3/6/15 [sig]
	3		No 13 pr. Ammn. to be drawn for Rockhead till further orders. Lieut. W.O. Carpenter granted extension of leave until 7th inst. Comm. to FLAMERTINGHE issued. 27000 AAA to SA Section 720 VPKH " "	[sig]
				3CR 1/1699
	4		The roads (i) ST OMER - STAPLE - LES CISEAUX (ii) AIRE - HAZEBROUCK to be kept clear for the movement of the 13th Division.	ADSvy 434/15
			c/ H.S.M. Base to 20th Div. Supply Col. 120 Very Pistols to SA Section 40 Reflector Hand Grenades No.6 to SA Section 60 Rifle Grenades DVB Section	[sig]

Army Form C. 2118.

WAR DIARY
or
INTELLIGENCE SUMMARY.
(Erase heading not required.)

Instructions regarding War Diaries and Intelligence Summaries are contained in F.S. Regs., Part II. and the Staff Manual respectively. Title pages will be prepared in manuscript.

Place	Date	Hour	Summary of Events and Information	Remarks and references to Appendices
Molique	5		Leave of absence granted. Capt Wilkins & 4 men departed by evening train.	A+946.
			Lt Campbell leave extended to 7th inst.	WO112/anc/ 1504
			Provision of Hypo-Sulphate of Soda presently affording reasonable economy	HD5+J 524/15 [initials]
"	6		Thirteen men transferred to 1st Can Supply Column. Loaders received from Base ~~Havre~~ M.T. Depot HAVRE Depôt. Coins	
			Major Hills takes over duty of O.C. A.S.C. from Major [Grove?]	
	7		Base Chambers maintenance	
			Surcharges noted see GRO 507 3rd Jan 1915.	GRO476
			Indians are not to be carried on Government vehicles	GRO480 " 481
			Each Office NCO shall have 100th Tables 47 gauge received	[initials]

1577 Wt. W10791/1773 500,000 1/15 D.D.&L. A.D.S.S./Forms/C. 2118.

WAR DIARY
or
INTELLIGENCE SUMMARY.
(Erase heading not required.)

Army Form C. 2118.

Place	Date	Hour	Summary of Events and Information	Remarks and references to Appendices
Morgreve	8th		Purchased iron Krans D's to carry picks extract on each lorry.	SSO 1012/45
			More Inspection Genderous receptacles north of Belle	
			Estimating Committee formed at G.H.Q. for purpose of receiving investigating inventions.	A A & R M G 9/1/736 CJm
			Instructions issued Tank mortars to Brigades as follows	
			6th Cav. Bde — 2	
			7 " " 3	
			8 " " 3	
	9		Capt Williams Lept Kitchen & B. has returned from leave	MAR M.G. 1/1750 CJm
			& the 2PM train from Victoria.	
			Received Control orders for 1st Army area.	
			All men inoculated in the company except 2 Farriers	
			42000.SA.RHGuard	
			96 Travel Hostel Bouls 6 7 Siv Bde.	

WAR DIARY or INTELLIGENCE SUMMARY

Army Form C. 2118.

(Erase heading not required.)

Place	Date	Hour	Summary of Events and Information	Remarks and references to Appendices
MORBECQUE	10		Answer received re having a RAMC Colonel. Not allowed.	ADMS 2431
			5" incendiary shells transferred from Ammunition Col. to STRAZEELE	
			Return re: ammunition received to collect 4 Stokes Mortars from 9th Inf. Bde.	DAA & QMG
			3500g .303 Ball yes 276 Webley Pistol & Revolver yes	
			18 Trench Mortar Bomb 5" Ensor yes 48 Lewis MG Links 6th Bn Bde.	Cfw
			75,000g .303 B Tracer yes 16 " " RH Gas	
			18 .13000 Vickerian MG Flare 16 Ensor yes	
			50,000g .301 Trench Mortar Flare " "	
			16 670 Cliffs	
			Received 2 Stokes Mortars from 6th York Regt.	
	11		Permission for Admission to the Camel School GHQ with a view	APC 352/15
			to being granted a temporary Commission in the Infantry.	
			Copy taken	
			Motor cycles with damaged frames to H.V. will be exchanged	GRO 9001
			on application being made O/C Supply Column	GRO 898
			Reserve to be made of spares from Canada from Base	
			Stationery Depot.	
			Purchase of Spare Parts to be submitted to ADGSAT for approval	ODS17 523/15
			Proposed War 14th Dept G are made Supply.	Cfw

Army Form C. 2118.

WAR DIARY
or
INTELLIGENCE SUMMARY.
(Erase heading not required.)

Instructions regarding War Diaries and Intelligence Summaries are contained in F. S. Regs., Part II. and the Staff Manual respectively. Title pages will be prepared in manuscript.

Place	Date	Hour	Summary of Events and Information	Remarks and references to Appendices
MorBECQUE	13 C		Officer acting Remt. W. Court Martial Orders being in Base Post Offices with rates most refer to Base Somewhere prior Departure on return	Recc 354/15
			Interpreter issued on the care of our time of year cont in others on a light blue gorps field	3CD 11/7 69
"	13		1 NCO & 3 men become on leave of 8.33 PM from HAZEBROUCK At N.O. letter Satads 1/2018 when a soldier is transferred to first Employ when a warrant is granted him young married men proceeding on leave	ACC 344/15
			Pst. DRo 439 Strength returned Branch Rec. office of SSO by 9 PM Friday. Purchase return by 9 PM Saturday Number of Rifles short see Repaid with number of long & short bayonets unit required by DADOS, 3CD.	3CD NO1/7/80 SSO/7019/15 DADOS 14/1 Cfee

WAR DIARY or INTELLIGENCE SUMMARY

Army Form C. 2118.

Place	Date	Hour	Summary of Events and Information	Remarks and references to Appendices
MORBECQUE	14		No more vehicles are to be sent to Corps H.Q. Workshops at STEENBECQUE without reference to DADOS.	DRO 498
	15		Captain Whyte, officer in charge of branch requisition office No 3. No 1 hand grenades to be issued to R.F. & R.E's. No 1 hand grenades to be issued to R.E's only. Capt. Davis returns from leave on 21/6/15. 50 hand mortar bombs RA 920, 4000 · 303 to 2 R.E's	DRO 500 Cpln.
			In cases where an carrier is provided on each side of the lorry, that on the off hand side is to be employed only for tools. That also on rifle for oil, waste and flare (also to be painted black with a white "W" or "O" on both sides)	D.of T. Douinlad Mem: 88
			Ref. DRO 404. Return of motor cycles 2. Nil. hand mortar Bombs 62 H.A. C.B. 50 trench mortar Bombs 3000 · 303 Steinoke Yeomanry month	DRO 501
	16.		Notification of G.O.C's visit at 10.30 A.M. Memorandum re casualties. A copy of return of motor cycles also sent to OC am C. Original e/o envelope 1st Royal DSS. on 13th of each month. 50 trench mortar Bombs to 1st Royal DSS	3CDN O1/ 1432. Cpln.

WAR DIARY
or
INTELLIGENCE SUMMARY.
(Erase heading not required.)

Army Form C. 2118.

Place	Date	Hour	Summary of Events and Information	Remarks and references to Appendices
HQ B.E.F.	16.		Wire from ADS+T to collect two 3 Ton Lorries from GHQ Corks to supply Column.	CfM
"	17		Received Lorries from GHQ Troops Supply Col. Escorted by Maj. Gen: Briggs GOC 3rd Can. Div. Inspected by " " 303 6SA Ration RHA 64000 13 p.m. to 13 p.m. 500 " "	CfM
			Range to exist. Destruction of grass land the avenue	GRO 514
			Officers commanding units are authorised to issue passes to M. Ouise.	GRO 516 GRO 518
"	18		Extension of service must be notified to OMG 3rd Echelon.	ADS+T 4-31/15
			Re: Monthly return of Officers; Officers serving with MT Units attached to Workshops to be noted on return.	
			Memoranda re numerical class list, clerks marked with compass "A" non depot to OC Base MT Dept. REB page 7 p.	GRO 362/13 CfM

1268 Hand Grenade Mills 577 12 D 95 | 3000-303 63rd D55
500 Heights 1st 13th Ration RHA | 6 Hand Grenades Mills 577 12 D 95
500 63rd D95 French Bombs

Army Form C. 2118.

WAR DIARY
or
INTELLIGENCE SUMMARY.
(Erase heading not required.)

Instructions regarding War Diaries and Intelligence Summaries are contained in F. S. Regs., Part II. and the Staff Manual respectively. Title pages will be prepared in manuscript.

Place	Date	Hour	Summary of Events and Information	Remarks and references to Appendices
MORBECQUE	19		Brassards are not to be worn on War Dept. Vehicles	GRO 920
			Drivers of M.T. vehicles. Formation Railhead the latest.	GRO 923
			Civilian articles of clothing may not be worn on any account. On duty. Chin straps the worn down.	"The"
			Report returned on Macintoshs types still obtained & pleased	Port. 584/5 Q/A
	20		Capt. Davies ordered to H.Q. R.F.C. for orders. 2/Lt. Ritchie to before him	A.R.C 318/15
			Lorry Casualty Book written up to date.	
			All units of division warned to scarce 4 6 PM 22nd inst. to return full motor cars tonnie & cycles on charge on 19 inst.	G.R.s 520
			Officers when mounted & away from their Hotels must wear Sam Browne belts with cross belts	G.R.s 523 Q/A.

1577 Wt. W10791/1773 500,000 1/15 D. D. & L. A.D.S.S./Forms/C. 2118.

WAR DIARY
or
INTELLIGENCE SUMMARY.
(Erase heading not required.)

Army Form C. 2118.

Place	Date	Hour	Summary of Events and Information	Remarks and references to Appendices
Noirefontaine	21		Details of Railway Pay received for APO in Old & New Army. Fuel wood can still be husbanded & drawn from the Forest of Nieppe where it is cut ready for drawing.	
	22		Capt Davis returned from leave arriving Boulogne at 6 P.M. 6 Hand Grenades Mills to D.H.Q's. Capt Davis A.S.C. proceeded to H.Q RFC to report for duty. Lt. R. Kirke arrived for duty from 2nd A.d. Div. Supply Col. No blank o white paint available whereas AOD. approval to purchase locally not allowed.	GR 941
"	23		2 Log Books for each MT vehicle & both 2 Repair books for each " " " " " " Motor Lorries rear tabs to be marked on bowie sheets in white figures. For Cars 4" left 5/8" wide 6" " 5/8" " N.O members of letters on back or Eqpt. The registration number 993 Renault 13 1/4" H.E. 2573 P.r Peston RMA	GRO 944

Place	Date	Hour	Summary of Events and Information	Remarks and references to Appendices
HORSBECQUE	23		When vegetables are purchased the particular kind never always to be shown so to base lots, both R.A.S.C.	SSO/1020 Oper /s/
"	24		Approval granted Army nominal for fittol canning	Yes
			Lt. Keith proceed on leave of absence	
	25		Received reports from the carried details on offhand rail, that him will be hauled service cobon. On the night had rest will be on tin of oil some of water; the latter hauled lines with a large W & O' Creek respectively. 2 is each swore petrol be carried under the lorries.	MD&T 559/15
			Full Corbs Staff to be collected returned to Ammunition or Supply Railheads	D.R.O. First
			When auto cycles is are lost or stolen a note will be to furnish to (a) application to Army & Corps Rodin Orders. Application will also to (b) A.P.M. of Division or Corps. of Rent 15:- (a) OC are or DOO according as whether the loss affects the Ad & or AOD.	D.R.O. S&O

Army Form C. 2118.

WAR DIARY
or
INTELLIGENCE SUMMARY.
(Erase heading not required.)

Instructions regarding War Diaries and Intelligence Summaries are contained in F. S. Regs., Part II. and the Staff Manual respectively. Title pages will be prepared in manuscript.

Place	Date	Hour	Summary of Events and Information	Remarks and references to Appendices
MORBECQUE	26		Hand grenade Bombs in future are not to be returned to Railhead Men to be in billets by 9 P.M.	O.T. Grace 4462
			The Officer or NCO in charge of a convoy of motor lorries which is having through an area occupied by the French Army will inform all French sentries that he is in charge of the convoy & request them to permit the whole of the vehicles to pass.	ADS+J 959
				J/m
	27		Anyone found damaging crops will be severely dealt with	920 Sd.8
			Casualties affecting O.d.C. Personnel to be reported to OC auc as they occur	651
			6 milo H Grenades S Pork Company	J/m

1577 Wt. W10791/1773 500,000 1/15 D. D. & L.   A.D.S.S./Forms/C. 2118.

Army Form C. 2118.

WAR DIARY
or
INTELLIGENCE SUMMARY.

(Erase heading not required.)

Instructions regarding War Diaries and Intelligence Summaries are contained in F. S. Regs., Part II. and the Staff Manual respectively. Title pages will be prepared in manuscript.

Place	Date	Hour	Summary of Events and Information	Remarks and references to Appendices
MORBECQUE	28		Reinoculation of men who have only had one dose of Anti-typhoid serum to commence at once	ADMS Z 398/6
			Return of Grenade to reach AA & QMG by 12 Noon on 29th	
			2 L/Dukes granted extension of leave till 1st July	ADS₃ 621/15
			Train & Boat arrangements from CALAIS 4.30 PM FOLKESTONE 6.0 PM	3 CD S/S 1/2.0 Oct
			9000.303 to Royal Naval Recon	
			49000.303	
"	29		Started making trays for petrol tins. 5 bins on left hand side of vehicle & 2 on right. These latter to oil small hand is black with white 'O'. 'N' painted on.	G/...
			49000.303 to Royal Naval Dock	

1577 Wt. W10791/1773 500,000 1/15 D. D. & L. A.D.S.S./Forms/C. 2118.

Army Form C. 2118.

WAR DIARY
or
INTELLIGENCE SUMMARY.
(Erase heading not required.)

Instructions regarding War Diaries and Intelligence Summaries are contained in F. S. Regs., Part II. and the Staff Manual respectively. Title pages will be prepared in manuscript.

Place	Date	Hour	Summary of Events and Information	Remarks and references to Appendices
MORBECQUE	June 30		Received 100 lbs of service fat from Ordnance sufficient for about 9 lorries.	
			Question from A.D.O.S. re amount & weight of gunparts carried in park. Answered by reference to G.1090/SS Sept 1914.	A.D.S./Q 626
			Ammunition receipts to to-date :—	?
			June	
			1st 50 Hand grenades No 1 from Rail Head STRAZEELE	
			48 " " 5 " " " "	
			75 " " 6 " " " "	
			240 V Pistol flares " " " "	
			2nd 27000 .303 " " " "	
			120 V Pistol Cartridges " " " "	
			4th 60 Rifle Grenades " " " "	
			40 Hand Grenade No 6 " " " "	
			120 V P Cartridges " " " "	
			7th 115000 " " " "	
			10th 202000 SA .303 " " " "	
			11th 10,000 " " " " " "	
			13th 4,000 " " " " " "	
			16th 3,000 " " " " " "	
			500 St Venant	

Army Form C. 2118.

WAR DIARY
or
INTELLIGENCE SUMMARY.
(Erase heading not required.)

Place	Date	Hour	Summary of Events and Information	Remarks and references to Appendices
Mokoges	June 18		Ammunition Receipts for Week	
	23		17000 .303 From Rhead STRAZEELE	
	26		993 HE 13/a " "	
			248 13/m Shap " "	
	27		404 HE 13/a " "	
	29		100 13/m Shot " "	
			40,000 .303 " "	gm

J Martin Capt. RoC
OC 3rd Co Ammn Park

3rd Cavalry Division.

18/6231

Confidential

War Diary

of

3rd Cav. Ammunition Park.

from 1st July 1915 to 31st July 1915.

(Volume V.)

WAR DIARY
or
INTELLIGENCE SUMMARY.
(Erase heading not required.)

Army Form C. 2118.

Place	Date	Hour	Summary of Events and Information	Remarks and references to Appendices
MORBECQUE	July 1		Postal Service. Letters posted before 12 Noon at 3rd CD box of the Mack London following morning. Re Supervision of Sentence act. The term of sentence sentenced is to be portion remainder or release from prison. Report to be sent in on Cards stat. this trial."	G720 556 acc 392/6 C/u
"	2		Personnel sent to Base will be provided with written orders showing their destination, place to report & reason for being sent down. Discharges on termination of Engagement under para 1 GRO 507 3rd Jan 1915 soldiers to be sent to Base depot of unit or formation 14 days before date due for discharge. NCO's & men proceeding on leave to take arms with them: ammunition etc. withdrawn at Base & returned on return. Will water not to be used for washing motor cars etc.	G.R.O. 975 " 976 " 980 G.R.O. 557

Army Form C. 2118.

WAR DIARY
or
INTELLIGENCE SUMMARY.
(Erase heading not required.)

Instructions regarding War Diaries and Intelligence Summaries are contained in F. S. Regs., Part II. and the Staff Manual respectively. Title pages will be prepared in manuscript.

Place	Date	Hour	Summary of Events and Information	Remarks and references to Appendices
MORBECQUE	July 2		Letter demanding note cars Topless Car…. it should be stated	ADS/y
			1. the unit to which car is issued	634
			2. the crew & has been sent to repair shop.	ADS/y
			Ordnance Officer of Hazebrouck may on authority of GOC hath local purchase up to £25 for stores & spares for repairs &c.	543/1
			Lt Col Williams will visit 4 trains via RE material to PLOEGSTEERT.	GS
"	3		Report on WD supply required.	CC
			Pocket lite made on left front of lorry be inspected re repairs or smoke helmet.	1933
			Claim cards of Forums & Stafford lorries not returned from — damages to Base MT Depot.	3CD 11/205 GS

Army Form C. 2118.

WAR DIARY
or
INTELLIGENCE SUMMARY.
(Erase heading not required.)

Instructions regarding War Diaries and Intelligence Summaries are contained in F. S. Regs., Part II. and the Staff Manual respectively. Title pages will be prepared in manuscript.

Place	Date	Hour	Summary of Events and Information	Remarks and references to Appendices
MORBECQUE	July 4		Leave Travis BOULOGNE 1 AM. Victoria 5 PM. Victoria 7.15 PM & 7.30 PM. Boulogne 11.30 PM. Ammunition return received checked & horses & found correct. Motor cycle bits marked with a cross & 3 CAP as well thus [sketch of crossed bars with 3 CAP]	C/M
"	5		Opened HE boxes with shrapnel inside found them correct. Having plans maps & lorries with stores in them cleared out & stores rearranged.	C/M

WAR DIARY
or
INTELLIGENCE SUMMARY.

(Erase heading not required.)

Army Form C. 2118.

Place	Date	Hour	Summary of Events and Information	Remarks and references to Appendices
MORBECQUE	July 6		Replacement of gear of 20 HP Daimler Cars. Coupled new rebirth diamond to replace any casualty. Owing to a new design in the sprocket two boxes procured to fit road junction 100x East of Strand T in PETIT PONT which is 2 miles S.E. of NEUVE EGLISE. They dumped RE 01500 returned	DSJ 3969/3 ANGMG 11/57 CJm
"	7		2nd Lt. W.O. Campbell proceeded on leave of absence for 14th 2nd Luck RFA returned from leave. Placed a control post for traffic at the end of MORBECQUE working in conjunction with the supply column posted at S end.	CJm
"	8		transferred to England with the convoy or without authority from HQ 3rd Car Divn.	GRO 565 CJm

Army Form C. 2118.

WAR DIARY
or
INTELLIGENCE SUMMARY.
(Erase heading not required.)

Instructions regarding War Diaries and Intelligence Summaries are contained in F. S. Regs., Part II. and the Staff Manual respectively. Title pages will be prepared in manuscript.

Place	Date	Hour	Summary of Events and Information	Remarks and references to Appendices
HOPBECQUE	9		Recommended Capt William Secemand Small Ammunition Park Lieut Campbell	ACC 403/15.
			of Siege Train kept to	
"	10		Capt Williams PLOEGSTEERT with the lorries returned RE Stores	
			Alteration in Ammunition to be carried in Park.	
			10 rounds p. gun for 500 mm of each regiment = 45000 rounds	3 CD / 2060
			6000 " " M machine Gun (26). = 156000 "	
			Total 201,000 Rounds	O/C
			Deficiencies in establishment of repair to be made up + duplicates consigned to Railhead.	

1577 Wt.W10791/1773 500,000 1/15 D. D. & L. A.D.S.S./Forms/C. 2118.

Army Form C. 2118.

WAR DIARY
or
INTELLIGENCE SUMMARY.
(Erase heading not required.)

Place	Date	Hour	Summary of Events and Information	Remarks and references to Appendices
MORBECQUE	10		From 13th inst. units drawing wood from NIEPPE must have an indent signed by Div. I.O. Receipt will be given G.H.Co. drawing Ft. wood. Indents received for N.C.O.s II Army, or BOSDOUCH or BONS MOYEN or BOIS D'AMONT. Officers leaving Chera or Bawd 9 France. Briefed in France. Bridge over Canal on HAZEBROUCK – SAINT VENANT road closed from 9 P.M. 12th to 4 A.M. on 13th.	520. 670. GR0571
	12		Completing issues/sick boot refixes.	
	13		S.A.A.ammunition G5c carried one own lorries 5 lorries sent to No 2 Res	

WAR DIARY
or
INTELLIGENCE SUMMARY.

(Erase heading not required.)

Army Form C. 2118.

Place	Date	Hour	Summary of Events and Information	Remarks and references to Appendices
MORBECQUE	14		HQ of Division moved as follows:—	G.R.O. 576
			GOC & GS to GRANDE BOIS	
			AA & QMG } to PIHEM	
			ADMS }	
			DADOS } to HEURINGHEM	
			ADVS }	
				G/M
"	15		Rations reached to rear figure 1¼ + 7 Mens ½ lb	GRO 580
			milk on tea 8 men	
			Board Jackson explained "	ADOS B/15
			Serum Vehicle Shower by 20 wt OC AC	
			Field Cashier moved to Marie BEARINGHEM.	
				W.O.C

WAR DIARY
or
INTELLIGENCE SUMMARY.

Army Form C. 2118.

Place	Date	Hour	Summary of Events and Information	Remarks and references to Appendices
MORBECQUE	16		Every person leaving GHQ must have a proper pass. Tools, materials re shown on Mobilization Store Tables never to exceed for Unit Advance.	GRO 1000
			Mustard ration is reduced from 50g to 30g from 8th inst.	GRO 1006 GRO 1007
			AB395 Face values not to be entered on original suspension receipts.	GRO 1008
			Officers are forbidden to make personal visits to the Base or Advanced Base MT Depots for spare parts unless a permit is obtained from A.D.S.T.	GRO 1009
			Lime Juice to "fill available on Sundays & holidays	1013
	17		Alterations for No 1 Hand Grease Gun to be applied against 25" Log Books arrived for the company for spares for mileage & petrol consumption	2RO 584
				— WQC

WAR DIARY
or
INTELLIGENCE SUMMARY.

Army Form C. 2118.

Place	Date	Hour	Summary of Events and Information	Remarks and references to Appendices
MORBECQUE	18		Vacuum 'A' oil will not be supplied in future. Sunda oils will be issued whilst Cav vehicles with steam valve engines. Whilst oil will be issued to motor lorries and to cycles. Pelican & mopeds require 4 Day	Day Y Corrections no 91 GM 20/7: 6434
"	19		Three lorries reported to Hd Qrs of 6th 7th & 8th Brigade at 12 noon on 20 G. A/CSM Bradford recommended for new armies. Corpl Kittel Ammunition Parks reorganised. Cavalry Amm Parks remain the same.	A1942 GRO 1524

W.N.C

WAR DIARY
or
INTELLIGENCE SUMMARY.

Army Form C. 2118.

Place	Date	Hour	Summary of Events and Information	Remarks and references to Appendices
MORBECQUE	20		Leave boat in future expects from BOULOGNE at 10 P.M.	GRO 1017
			Officers are not permitted to assess non-ished magazines W.D. chine	
			The conversion of temporary commission bypernanal will not be connected to the cessation of hostilities	C.C.
			Loopoal of rifles showed to retained there French mortar bombs should be returned to Amm -unition Park. O.C. Amm Park to collect from units.	A.D.O.S. C.C. 363
	21		When submitting want for special signs of clothing movements to be given. Capt. C. J. Martin left on leave & returns for 168 hrs. Capt. A. R. Wham assuming	D.A.D.O.S. 18/7/15
	22		Trench Mortar Bombs not to be withdrawn from P.E. Amm Park. An of 2 Amm Park lorries sanctioned for conveying R.E. tools material from Park to working parties. One lorry sent to near ELVERDINGHE	A/2 P DADTMG

Army Form C. 2118.

WAR DIARY
or
INTELLIGENCE SUMMARY.
(Erase heading not required.)

Instructions regarding War Diaries and Intelligence Summaries are contained in F. S. Regs., Part II. and the Staff Manual respectively. Title pages will be prepared in manuscript.

Place	Date	Hour	Summary of Events and Information	Remarks and references to Appendices
MORBECQUE	Aug. 22		to deliver Supply Column lorry at present being used for their purposes. Return of vehicles transferred conveyed to 6 p.m. Saturday & read. A.D.S.T. every Sunday. Supplies & O.C. ASC. accpt in car of Mr returns Central Park say to establish at discretion of A.P.M. Parcos sent to stnn.	D.R.O. 595.
	23		A pplication for commission to staff white officers in in reg. engagement in rmk. Trnsfr. when hostility, to have seniority shown.	D.R.O. 596. D.R.O. 599
			2.Lr. R.N. Stevens joined from R.N. & Trnsp Suppl Column for duty. Route ARCQUES – AIRE – WALLONCAPPEL – THIENNES – HAZEBROUCK – MORBECQUE – ST. VENANT k.k. hoff char for 19th Div.	
			Leave Train attend BOULOGNE 0.08 HAZEBROUCK 4.00	D.R.O. 601
	24		Capt A P Williams left for England to report for duty at W.O. Refurner B/2055 of 13/7/15 applies equally to blans of T.F. 2 Lieut R.H Stevens posted to No 2 Section.	O.C. ASC 448/75 O.C. ASC 435/15 W.O.C

Army Form C. 2118.

WAR DIARY
or
INTELLIGENCE SUMMARY.
(Erase heading not required.)

Instructions regarding War Diaries and Intelligence Summaries are contained in F. S. Regs., Part II. and the Staff Manual respectively. Title pages will be prepared in manuscript.

Place	Date	Hour	Summary of Events and Information	Remarks and references to Appendices
MERBECQUE	July 25		Received about 2000 S.A.A. MARK VII from 3 Cav Supply Col also box of Webley pistol ammunition which were returned to Railhead. Received Triumph motor cycle frame No 255938 Engine No 36607 from 3 Cav Sup Supply Col without tools spares &c to replace bike frame No 255498.	
	26		O.C. ASC abandon cars to report to O.C. R.H.A. for duty for our work. Started Sunbeam Car No 1815. Received notice that tyre forces at Hazebrouck would shortly be moved. Meanwhile tyre presses at ISBERGUES & STRAZEELE would remain available. Received notice from A.S.M.S. that such in future was not to be used but a pit & grass catcher was to be used. This was done.	SofT 6577
	27		Received notice that ration numbers were to be in by noon each Thursday J.A. & QMG 3 Corps instructed that as Capt Martin should be invited to attend report. Lory No 3 returned from ELVERDINGE with motor superstructure.	

1577 Wt.W10791/1773 500,000 1/15 D. D. & L. A.D.S.S./Forms/C. 2118.

Army Form C. 2118.

WAR DIARY
or
INTELLIGENCE SUMMARY.
(Erase heading not required.)

Place	Date	Hour	Summary of Events and Information	Remarks and references to Appendices
MORBECQUE	July 28		Started Lorry No 5 I section to ELVERDINGHE in place of Lorry No 3 I section. Received Douglas cycle No 21732 (frame) in place of Triumph Cycle No 255938 returned as useless.	
			Received authority to treat second Lorry to ELVERDINGHE Sent Bareham Car No 1812 to BOULOGNE to meet Capt Martin Airport	OC ASC
"	29		Started Lorry No 3 I section for duty at ELVERDINGE. Left at 6 am Capt. Martin returned from leave.	
	30		Lt Salter signed an agreement for permission 1 our resort 6 months leave. In future when wanted by Lithot can be produced by Officers & men when travelling on leave, they will be required to pay full fare. They proceed at rate of 400 per person will be issued in future in future as below.	A.g. B/2153- R.O. 617 R.O. 616
			R67 books to be kept in future as below.	W.O.C

DATE	JOURNEY	TOTAL MILES	TIME OUT	TIME IN	OFFICER USING CAR	PETROL RECEIVED	PETROL CONSUMED	MILES PER GAL TO 2 PLACES DECIMALS

Army Form C. 2118.

WAR DIARY
or
INTELLIGENCE SUMMARY.

(Erase heading not required.)

Place	Date	Hour	Summary of Events and Information	Remarks and references to Appendices
MORBECQUE	July 31		One pair of motor goggles per man can be issued to Drivers Instructors OC. Claims for damage of brought horses to individuals concerned to be dealt with by O.C. as matter of instructions. Return of August for horses to be taken as return 3/9	G.R.O 1044 G.R.O 1036

W.O.C.

WAR DIARY or INTELLIGENCE SUMMARY

Army Form C. 2118.

Instructions regarding War Diaries and Intelligence Summaries are contained in F. S. Regs., Part II. and the Staff Manual respectively. Title pages will be prepared in manuscript.

(Erase heading not required.)

Place	Date	Hour	Summary of Events and Information	Remarks and references to Appendices

Issues

Date	No:	To whom issued	Nature	Remarks
MORBECQUE July 5	14,000	S.A. ScT R.H.A.	.303 S.A.	
6	828	8" B? Am Col	Pistol Webley	
7	1800	Leicesters	.303 S.A.	
8	100	K Battery R.H.A.	Woolwich Bombs 3·7	
"	100	C " "	"	
"	35	R.H. Guards	"	
"	35	10th Hussars	"	
"	30	Essex Yeo	"	
10	32,000	8" B? Am Col	.303 S.A.	
12	276	8 Cav B? HQ	Pistol Webley	
"	19,000	N.S. Yeo	.303 S.A.	
"	7,000	1" Royal Dragoons	.303 S.A.	
"	46,000	1" Life Gds	.303 S.A.	
"	10,000	2" " "	"	
"	58,000	Am Col	"	

Receipts

Date	No:	Received from	Nature	
July 5	14,000	(Railway)	.303 S.A.	
8	300	"	Woolwich Bombs 3·7	
"	828	"	Pistol Webley	
"	18,000	"	.303 S.A.	
"	700	"	13 PR. H.E.	
10	32,000	"	.303 S.A.	
12	13,000	Royal Horse Sqn	.303 S.A.	
12	2,000	3 Royal Sc?	.303 S.A.	
"	712	Amm. Col	13 P.R. QF Shp.	
13	712	(Railway)	13 P.R. QF H.E.	
"	80,000	Amm Col	.303 S.A.	
18	54,000	Essex Yeo	.303 S.A.	
20	100	K Battery	"	
"	100	C "	"	
"	4·8	K "	Woolwich Bombs 3·7	
"	5·0	C "	Trench Bombs ·95	W.O.C

WAR DIARY or INTELLIGENCE SUMMARY

Army Form C. 2118.

Place	Date	Hour	Issues				Receipts				Remarks and references to Appendices
			No Rounds	To Whom issued	Nature	Remarks	Date	No Rounds	To whom issued	Nature	
MORBECQUE	July 12"		712	Amm Col	13 P.R. HE		July 18 "	96	Railhead	13 P.R. HE	
	13		8,000	Lincolor Regt	.303 S.A.		20	1,068	Amm. Col	13 P.R. Shrap.	
	"		828	"	Pistol Webley		21	456	Railhead	13 P.R. HE	
	"		697	Railhead	13 P.R. Shrap		25	828	"	Pistol Webley	
	"		404,000	"	.303 S.A.		24	10,000	73 G. A.C.C.	.303 Mk VII	Err.
	15		2,000	10" Hussars	"		"	2,000	"	.303 Mk VI	Err.
	19		32,000	Railhead	"		26	5,000	Railhead	.303 S.A.	
	"		1,068	Amm Col	13 P.R. HE		"	552	"	Pistol Webley	
	21		1,440	Railhead	13 P.R. Shrap		"	892	"	13 P.R. Shrap	
	22		1,000	Royal Hors.S.A	.303 S.A.		31"	35	Royal Hors. S.A.	Woolwich Bomb 3.7	
	23		4,000	2" Life G.ds	"		"	6,000	Railhead	.303 S.A.	
	"		8,000	1st Royal Dragns	"		"	892	"	13 P.R. HE	
	25		552	H.Q. Cav Bgde	Pistol Webley						
	"		7,000	Railhead	.303 S.A.	Err.					
	"		2,000	"	S.A. MARK VI	Err.					W.O.E

Army Form C. 2118.

WAR DIARY
or
INTELLIGENCE SUMMARY.
(Erase heading not required.)

Instructions regarding War Diaries and Intelligence Summaries are contained in F. S. Regs., Part II. and the Staff Manual respectively. Title pages will be prepared in manuscript.

Place	Date	Hour	No of Rounds	To Whom Issued	Nature	Remarks
MORBECQUE	Feb					
	28"		105 lbs	Railhead	Black Powder	
	30"		9,000	Leicester Yeo	.303 SA	
	31"		892	Railhead	13 P.R. Shrap.	

Summary of Events and Information | Remarks and references to Appendices

W.O. Campbell Lt.
for OC 2nd Ammn Park

1577 Wt.W10791/1773 500,000 1/15 D. D. & L.   A.D.S.S./Forms/C. 2118.

121/6598

3rd Cavalry Division

Confidential

War Diary

of

3rd 10 ar. Ammn Park.

From 1st August 1915 to 31st August 1915

(Volume 1).

WAR DIARY
INTELLIGENCE SUMMARY
(Erase heading not required.)

Army Form C. 2118

Place	Date	Hour	Summary of Events and Information	Remarks and references to Appendices
MORBECQUE	August 1st		Took kit inspection. Point of Crossbars to be Stop and Down for new repair brush. Took necessary steps re Tin & another helmets.	CC 14/8
	2		No more Klaxon horns to be demanded. There is only to be issued to J.U.C.s or my senior officers. Started the Vardaris lorries for moving. All lorries sent in to Chains etc. Various reports on postponing move until 4th inst. Orders received for postponing move until 4th inst.	DQT 6754 O.C. ASC
	3		Captain Martin recommended 2L W.A. Campbell & 2LT W. Kerl for promotion. Letters received that Field Cashier will discharge french upto for which 500 at rate of 26 frs 65 cts to the £. Issued instrs. to this effect. Took various steps in consultation with O.C. Workshops to comply with DQT Circular 97 re Economy.	ADQ&T 839/1 W.O.C.

WAR DIARY
or
INTELLIGENCE SUMMARY.
(Erase heading not required.)

Army Form C. 2118

Place	Date	Hour	Summary of Events and Information	Remarks and references to Appendices
	August			
MORBECQUE	4		Moved Park from MORBECQUE at 11 am. to ENQUIN LES MINES arrived 1.30. Went round all billets & lines were all correct & clear. Parked lorries. No 1 section on main road. No 2 section on ESTRE BLANCHE road. H.Q. letc. Workshops in school yard. Field Officer, cook shop. Latrines.	
ENQUIN LES MINES.	5		Inspected & found billets for Officers & 2. C.O.s (Sergts. only) Fitches Marquee for workshops staff.	
	6		Arranged for M.O. from 3 Field Squadron at Park. Visited by M.O. who inspected lines reported all correct. Fixed up bath in village from river. Lorries No 3 + 5 W section returned from ELVERDINGE. Billets to be visited monthly & lines per week.	R.O. 636 W.O.C.

WAR DIARY
or
INTELLIGENCE SUMMARY.
(Erase heading not required.)

Army Form C. 2118

Place	Date	Hour	Summary of Events and Information	Remarks and references to Appendices
ENQUIN LES MINES	August 7		Sent Lorry No 3 II Sect to be repaired (Gov No 3204) with wheel from No 7 II Sect (Gov No 8592) to ISJBERG. Visited LAIRES & District to see if it would be possible to put them. Found it quite impossible owing to bad roads & no water. Visited WITTERNES & QUERNES for circular pumping. Found them also impossible owing to no place for workshops & no road. Reported same to A.A. & Q.M.G.	
	8"		Instructed that we were not to move but to claim area with 10 Armoury Reading room opened in Schoolroom 12 noon to 9 p.m.	
	9"		R.A. Officer reported that he had finished exchanging unserviced H.E. 13 P.R. for serviced H.E. 13 P.R. between Batteries & Amm" Col. Canteen opened under Lt. Kuck R.F.A. Hours hours for Canteen as follows Sunday 12-2 pm — 6 pm — 9 pm Wed & Sat 12 to 9 pm. Other days 12 to 2 pm 4.30 pm to 9 pm	W.C.

WAR DIARY or INTELLIGENCE SUMMARY

Army Form C. 2118

Place	Date	Hour	Summary of Events and Information	Remarks and references to Appendices
ENQUIN LES MINES	Aug 10th		e.ff Stations with two lorries Nos 3 & 8. II Sect proceeded to Amm- Col to draw 25 R.H.A. gun fuses & then proceeded with 24 men also from there in the lorry. Bus to LA MOTTE to cut wattles for trenches returning there. Fixed area with 10th Division & arranged likely in conformity therewith Sect instructor to MORBECQUE to arrange clean with M. Bottin. Chum amounts to 54 francs for coal from November to May 1st 1915. Bathing parade.	a.a & B.M.G. 1/1596.
		2 pm	Letters of appointments in turn of formn. to U.S. in highest. Arranged with M.O. 10th Division to attend him July 11 am Circular re turn of pound received.	ec. 1420/2
	11"		Lorry with rations to Sisters at LA MOTTE. Received circular with reference to treatment of Amm- Parks in Divisional trops & Corp Troops. Lorry with rations to LA MOTTE. Closing of Estaminets extended to 8.30 pm	O.C.

Army Form C. 21

WAR DIARY
or
INTELLIGENCE SUMMARY.
(Erase heading not required.)

Instructions regarding War Diaries and Intelligence Summaries are contained in F. S. Regs., Part II. and the Staff Manual respectively. Title pages will be prepared in manuscript.

Place	Date	Hour	Summary of Events and Information	Remarks and references to Appendices
ENGUIN LES MINES	Aug 12		Lorry with rations to LA MOTTE. Battery Parade 2 pm. Detailed Car no 1615 for use of O.C. A.S.C. for day.	
	13"		Lorry with rations + 40 Gals Petrol + 4 Subs Vel to LA MOTTE. Fort drill 2 pm. Motor Cycle No 1 returned to S.O. 6th Brigade.	
	14"		Visited 100 battery return at LA MOTTE. I arranged to send another lorry. Lorry with rations to LA MOTTE.	
	15		Detailed lorries No 6 + 10 H.Q Sect + No 7 II Sect to LA MOTTE in place of Nos 3 + 5 II Sect. Detailed lorries No 5 H.Q Sect + 6.2 Sect to ARMETIERES.	W.M.C

WAR DIARY
or
INTELLIGENCE SUMMARY.

(Erase heading not required.)

Army Form C. 2118

Instructions regarding War Diaries and Intelligence Summaries are contained in F. S. Regs., Part II. and the Staff Manual respectively. Title pages will be prepared in manuscript.

Place	Date	Hour	Summary of Events and Information	Remarks and references to Appendices
ENQUIN LES MINES	Aug 16	2pm	Long with return to LA MOTTE Rifle Drill	
	17	2pm	Long with return to LA MOTTE Battery parade	
	18	2pm	Long with return to LA MOTTE Return trans train leaves CHARING CROSS at 8.50 am after Aug 23.	R.U. 679
	19	2pm	Long with return to LA MOTTE Battery parade	
	20	2pm	Exchanged H.E. for Shrapnel with fulminia. Long with return to LA MOTTE Rifle Drill In future 96 H.E. & 54 Shrapnel per gun to be carried	W.M.C

WAR DIARY
or
INTELLIGENCE SUMMARY.
(Erase heading not required.)

Army Form C. 2118

Place	Date	Hour	Summary of Events and Information	Remarks and references to Appendices
ENQUIN LES MINES	Aug 21		Corp No 6 I Sect hit by shell at ARMENTIERES. No casualties. Corp reports still unreadable.	
	22		Corp with rations to LA MOTTE	
		10.30 AM	Sanitary Car No 1615 Returned for work with O.C. A.S.C 3 Cavalry Div. Got L/Corp Cameron from G3 & reported to prints. Lorries No 8, 4, 2, 1 2nd Sect No 7 H.Q Sect & No 1, 2 & 6 Sanitary went for final run. Sgt in Charge reports all well Corp with rations to LA MOTTE	
	23		Corp with rations to LA MOTTE Motor agreement to hire field for vacation at 5 francs per week Rifle drill	
	24	2pm	Corp with rations to LA MOTTE Battery Parade	
		2pm	Corp No 3 II Sect returns for LA MOTTE with out Lorries (Apres) to have motor Cycle with S.O at ARMENTIERES for further period	W.M.C

WAR DIARY
or
INTELLIGENCE SUMMARY.

(Erase heading not required.)

Army Form C. 21

Place	Date	Hour	Summary of Events and Information	Remarks and references to Appendices
ENGUIN LES MINES.	AUG 25		Lewis no 3 & 7. 2" sent out to ISBERG for new types. Officer out to obs through echelons will not be shown off strength until instructions received to do so.	
	26	2pm	Lorry with ration to LA MOTTE. Returning found Sent Corp's dwelt to advanced section at LA MOTTE. He reported no arrival his Lorry who had this one.	S.R.S 701
		11.15pm	Guard reports that aircraft found OUR going in northerly direction. Shooting of guns absolutely prohibited.	
	27	2pm	Lorry with ration to LA MOTTE. Fort Douth. Estaminets to be open 11-1pm & 6 to 8pm.	GRO.11 WDC

WAR DIARY or INTELLIGENCE SUMMARY

Army Form C. 2118

Place	Date	Hour	Summary of Events and Information	Remarks and references to Appendices
ENQUIN LES MINES	AUG 28		ADS&T visited Park & directed a summary of petrol and cordage men to be sent up every day to return. He also gave orders that no cap of bicycles was to be sent without his sanction. 2 Lieut Stevens returned with war outfit & party from LA MOTTE. Also Corp. No 6 H.Q. urgently asking to return to Stiring. Running Lorries handed over to Capt. Jenner R.E. paid out Cox.	
	29		Sent Corp. No 4 II Sect to LA MOTTE to replace Corp No 6 H.Q. 2/Lt KIRKE went to ARMENTIERES & LA MOTTE & inspects all our Lorries which are carrying ammn. Arranged with SSO to return turn with Lorries at ARMENTIERES. O.C. A Sec 3 Cov Div inspects Park. 2/Lt Stevens went on leave for 168 hours	
	30	2 pm	ADMS 3 Cav Div inspects sanitary arrangements of Park & expressed approval. Rifle Drill & inspection of ammn. Men preceding on leave to take their rifles but not ammunition.	G.R.O. 1110 WCC

WAR DIARY or INTELLIGENCE SUMMARY

Army Form C. 2118

Place	Date	Hour	Summary of Events and Information	Remarks and references to Appendices
ENQUIN LES MINES	AUG 31	2 p.m.	Bethune Patrol. Lorries engaged in changing ammunition.	
	AUG		Summary of Issues of Ammunition during month	
			No of Rounds / To whom issued / Nature of Ammunition	
			1656 — Essex Yeomanry — Webley Pistol	
			2000 — 10th Royal Hussars — .303 S.A.	
			Receipts of Ammunition: Nil	

W.O. Campbell Lieut A.S.C.
for O.C. 3 Cav Div Amm. Park 31/8/15

3rd Cavalry Division

121/6973

Confidential

War Diary.

3rd Cav. Ammunition Park.

From 1st September 1915
To 30th September 1915.

(Volume 6.)

WAR DIARY
or
INTELLIGENCE SUMMARY.
(Erase heading not required.)

Army Form C. 2

Place	Date	Hour	Summary of Events and Information	Remarks and references to Appendices
ENQUIN LES MINES	SEPTEMBER 1		Stable hour from Nos 1, 2, 5, 6 with 8 asc Divn, 1 ASC & Co & RFA & 1 RCO RFA to be attached to 15th Sub Amm. Park at AUCHEL for orders. With 5 Battery RHA. The Amn Carry 572 13 PRHE & 328 Shrapnel. 5 Battery Amn Col will be at MOEUX LES MINES and 5 Battery guns at LES BREBINS. Monthly inspection of kilts 1½ Gallons of Paraffin per lamp to be used only	8/7195
	2	10.30	Bathing parade. Visited lorries at AUCHEL & arranged with O.C. 15 Sub Amm. Park that he should pay men there.	
		2 pm	Discharged Pte Salter Harris. Went on to CHOQUES & ascertained that 16th Amn Park is at STVENANT	672

WAR DIARY
or
INTELLIGENCE SUMMARY.
(Erase heading not required.)

Army Form C. 2118.

Instructions regarding War Diaries and Intelligence Summaries are contained in F. S. Regs., Part II. and the Staff Manual respectively. Title pages will be prepared in manuscript.

Place	Date	Hour	Summary of Events and Information	Remarks and references to Appendices
ENGUINEGATE MINES	3	2p	Handed over 7 lorries 2 R.Cos & 20 O.R. to 7" Amm Park 1st Corps. Amm Park with 1162 13PR HE & 648 13PR Shrapnel. 70ft Smith batteries	
	4	11a	Paid Coy	
		10.30a	Inf inspection	
		6.45p	The fun lorries of ASC to RE at ARMENTIERES returned	
	5		Sunbeam Car Astoryan to S.O. 6 Brigade came in here for overhaul.	
	6		2 Lt Strung returned from leave. 2/Field Select provision with G Battery, Am Col & select for C & K Battery Amm Col Motor cycle sent to S.O 6 Brigade returned. 2/Lt Strung joined 7" field Amm Park for ordnance duty with lorries.	W.O.C
	7	2p	Battery Parade. Bought Christmas for Wednesday next. 3 horses SOC	

WAR DIARY
or
INTELLIGENCE SUMMARY.

Army Form C. 2118

Place	Date	Hour	Summary of Events and Information	Remarks and references to Appendices
ENQUIN-LES MINES	SEPT 8		Thursday road with clinkers	
	9	2p	Sent Daimler Lorry No 6591 I ISJBERG to R.H.Tyres. Bathing Parade. Monday road with clinkers	
	10		Received lorry to various members of unit. a bus. Arranged to hire shed of Lumbrian Cars Record in AIRE	
	11		Installed Lorry No 4 & 2 Scot. to Army Gun parts for advanced section at ST VENANT. Sent Gun parts for adv d section at AUCHEL. Received orders to and list of stores surplus to Mobilisation establishment. Sent Cyclist L Cpl. Howard for service with G. Battery Ammn Col. to replace Pte. with broken cycle	

209

Army Form C. 2

WAR DIARY
or
INTELLIGENCE SUMMARY.
(Erase heading not required.)

Instructions regarding War Diaries and Intelligence Summaries are contained in F. S. Regs., Part II and the Staff Manual respectively. Title pages will be prepared in manuscript.

Place	Date	Hour	Summary of Events and Information	Remarks and references to Appendices
ENQUIN LES MINES	SEPT 12		Capt. Edwall wrote to Punch. Capt. Adams promoted to Capt. Received report as to what spares required for stamps in event of a war.	
		10.30	Tool Kit inspection	
		11 am	Paid out Coy.	
	13		Issued out our extra number helmets to AUCHEL detained section. Paid detained section at AUCHEL. On enquiring from A.A. & Q.M.G. replied that us could furnish 5 lorries for transport of garden bridge. ESTAMINET Ve MASSET LEROY placed out of bounds for Women.	DRO 736
	14	2p	Bathing parade. Repairs of Saunderson car for S.O. 6" Brigade completed. Amount of S.A.A. carried by this Park increased to 521,000. Informed A.A. & Q.M.G. that we could only furnish 3 lorries to carry bridge.	A30s Co VOC

Army Form C. 2118

WAR DIARY
or
INTELLIGENCE SUMMARY.
(Erase heading not required.)

Place	Date	Hour	Summary of Events and Information	Remarks and references to Appendices
ENQUIN LES MINES	SEPT 15		2 a S.O.S. 3 Cn/Sn visited Park & inspected top-covers. O/c inspected & mover general magazine & field reports.	
	16	2 pm	Started three empty lorries for work with 3 Field Squadron. Bathing parade. Received instructions re settlement of claims under 125 francs. Received instruction that we should under local arrangements for hire of room for empties stores in event of an advance. Made arrangements to hire cellar under mess room at 1 franc per week.	Aq+QMG 540/15 Aq+QMG 2662
	17	8 am 11:15 am 2/-	Started three empty lorries to report to 3rd Field Squadron at AIRES Station at 10.30 am. S/Sgt C. Ketchell left to join 356 Cy ASC at CALAIS. Sunbeam car 1813 returned by O.C. ASC with sundry defects. Advanced section from AUCHEL returned Advanced section from ST VENANT returned	WTC

Army Form C. 2118

WAR DIARY
or
INTELLIGENCE SUMMARY.
(Erase heading not required.)

Instructions regarding War Diaries and Intelligence Summaries are contained in F. S. Regs., Part II. and the Staff Manual respectively. Title pages will be prepared in manuscript.

Place	Date	Hour	Summary of Events and Information	Remarks and references to Appendices
ENQUIN LES MINES	Sept 18		Lorry No 3 set II to JISBERG for new tyres. A Corps. Workshop promoted to "A Sub". A Corps. Workshops. A Corps. Fatigue party thoroughly stored up workshop yard. No vehicles or papers arrived to-day.	
	19		Filled up C & B Batteries with 13 PR 44/80 fuzes. Filled up rest with same ammn for reserve. B.G. Bailey v B. Echelon	
	20		Started Photo ??? Capt Whitticks for duty with Ammn Col. Filled up Ammn Col with 13 PR 44/80 fuzes. Workshops repaired or turning in burning officer full refixing ready to serve. New type of smoke helmets issued or returned to replace old ones.	AA QMG 2748

60c

WAR DIARY
INTELLIGENCE SUMMARY
(Erase heading not required.)

Army Form C. 2118

Instructions regarding War Diaries and Intelligence Summaries are contained in F.S. Regs., Part II and the Staff Manual respectively. Title pages will be prepared in manuscript.

Place	Date	Hour	Summary of Events and Information	Remarks and references to Appendices
ENQUIN LES MINES	Sept. 21	12.10	Interview C/offs. Howard as & chat with 7 Brigade Amm. Col. Received notice that Amm. Col. for C & R Batteries were going to BOIS DE DAMES. Returning all mules 5 minutes to STRAZEELE. (sent to) Received orders that III Bgde R.H.A. Amm. Col. was at BOIS DE DAMES. Paid 109 Francs for Damage to return to report good. Settled all claims & inspected all billets for Damage. no further claim in this report.	
	22	10 am	Attached section of 7 Amm. Carriers 576 13 P.R.H.E. 324 B.P.R. Wheels and 174,000 S.A.A. + 24 O.R. 1 Officer for service with 7 Bgde Col. After receiving orders that this section was Posted at LE BREARDE or HAZEBROUCK 7 Bgde Amm Col reported they were at B of HAUT SCHOUBROUK East of the CISILVESTRE and FORET DE CLARMARAIS 5 A MAP G.C. ASC 3 Cos this wound at WESTREHEM. two Ammunition Railhead at LAPUGNOY	

Army Form C. 2118

WAR DIARY
or
INTELLIGENCE SUMMARY.
(Erase heading not required.)

Instructions regarding War Diaries and Intelligence Summaries are contained in F. S. Regs., Part II. and the Staff Manual respectively. Title pages will be prepared in manuscript.

Place	Date	Hour	Summary of Events and Information	Remarks and references to Appendices
AUCHEL	Sept 23	9.30 a.m.	Left ENGUIN LES MINES (Arrived) to AUCHEL pushed men Netwerk	
		9 a.m.	Inspected billets at ENGUIN before leaving & noted no damage.	
	24		Lorries engaged in changing B's a.a. at Chocques & Burgette. Built Cookhouse, re-arranged lorries etc. Drew 100 frames from Field Cashier for payment of	
	25		Paid out C/r. Sent return to 28 of S+T 1st Army. Lorries engaged in returning B's a.a. to CHOCQUES & LAPUGNOY. Completed hut for Cor 26 16/12.	
Nov. 26			Arm Lt (Inne) to ~~Knockroys~~ left but at Netwerk on Completed 44 HE 13 PR	W.D.C

1577 Wt.W10791/1773 500,000 1/15 D.D.&L. A.D.S.S./Forms/C. 2118.

WAR DIARY
or
INTELLIGENCE SUMMARY.
(Erase heading not required.)

Army Form C. 2118

Instructions regarding War Diaries and Intelligence Summaries are contained in F. S. Regs., Part II. and the Staff Manual respectively. Title pages will be prepared in manuscript.

Place	Date	Hour	Summary of Events and Information	Remarks and references to Appendices
AUCHEL	Sept 27		Supply Ration at NOEUX LES MINES Commenced in Bar Chambers H.Q Sect	
	28		2 Lieut Luck returned from Leave	
	29		Amm. Col moved to BOIS DE DAMES	
	30	2p	Rifle Inspection. Supply Rations Changed to LILLERS.	

WAR DIARY
or
INTELLIGENCE SUMMARY.

Army Form C. 2

Place	Date	Hour	Summary of Events and Information	Remarks and references to Appendices
ENQOIN LES MINES	Sept		Summary of Ammunition issued during month	
			No of Rounds / To Whom Issued / Nature of Ammunition	
	6		6000 / 10" Hussars / .303 S.A.	
	14		552 / " / Webly Pistol	
	"		276 / " / "	
	17		1000 / Leicester Yeo / .303 S.A.	
	18		39000 / Royal H.Gds. / "	
	18		39000 / Amm. Col. R.H.A / "	
	18		6000 / C. Battery R.H.A Amm Col / "	
	18		33000 / K " " " / "	
	"		552 / K " " " / Webly Pistol	
	19		828 / C " " " / "	
	"		71000 / K " " " / .303 S.A.	
	"		5000 / 1st Royal Dgs. / "	
	21		552 / 10" Hussars / Webly Pistol	

WAR DIARY
or
INTELLIGENCE SUMMARY.
(Erase heading not required.)

Army Form C. 2118

Place	Date	Hour	Summary of Events and Information	Remarks and references to Appendices
AUCHEL	Sept.		Issues Continued. Return of Ammunition	
			No. of Rounds	To Whom Issued		
	24		120	6th Cav Bde.	Cartridge Small Igniter	
	"		600	Amm. Col	"	
	"		360	Essex Yeo	"	
	"		480	6 Cav Bde	"	
	25		346	Amm Col	Mills Grenades	
	27		76	4th B: Amm Col	H.E. 44/60 13 P.R.	
	"		37000	"	Shrapnel 13 P.R.	Exchange
	28		80000	"	.303 S.A.	
	"		2760	"	Pistol Webley	
	29		152	"	13 P.R. H.E.	
	"		12	"	13 P.R. Shrapnel	
	"		23000	"	.303 S.A.	60C

WAR DIARY
or
INTELLIGENCE SUMMARY.

(Erase heading not required.)

Army Form C. 2118

Place	Date	Hour	Summary of Events and Information	Remarks and references to Appendices
ENQUIN LES MINES	Sept.		Summary of Ammunition Record during Month	
			Summary of Ammunition Record Return of Ammunition Received during Month	
		No. of Rounds	From whom Received	Nature of Ammunition	Remarks
	14	168000	Railhead Strazeele	.303 S.A.	
	18	52000	"	.303 S.A.	
	19	78000	"	"	
	"	552	"	Webley Pistol	
	21	50000	"	.303 S.A.	
	"	1380	"	Pistol Webley	
AUCHEL	23	1104	" LAPUGNOY	13 PR HE 44/80	recharges
	24	500	"	MILLS No 5 Grenades	
	24	480	"	"	
	25	192	"	Pistol Webley	
	"	1104	"	Very Pistol Cartridges	
	27	2200	"	"	
	30	3360	"	"	

WAR DIARY
or
INTELLIGENCE SUMMARY.
(Erase heading not required.)

Army Form C. 2118.

Place	Date	Hour	Summary of Events and Information	Remarks and references to Appendices
AUCHEL	Sept		Receipts continued	
			From Whom Received	
	27		Railhead LAPUGNOY	
	"		"	Return of Ammunition
	28		"	Pistol Webley 13 P.R. shrapnel
	"		"	13 B.P. H.E to .303 S.A
	30		"	Pistol Webley
	"		"	.303 S.A
	"		"	13 P.R Shrapnel
				" H.E

No of Rounds
28
37000
2760
8000
23000
12
128

Remarks
Receipts
Exchange
"
"
Exchange

W.O. Campbell Lieut
for O.C. 3 Cav Div Amm. Park
30-9-15.

3rd Cavalry Division

121/7496

No. 3. Cav. Ammo. Park

Dec. 15

Vol IX

Confidential

War Diary

of

3rd C.W. Ammunition Park

From 1st Oct 1915 to 31st Oct 1915

(Volume 9)

Army Form C. 2118.

WAR DIARY
or
INTELLIGENCE SUMMARY.
(Erase heading not required.)

Instructions regarding War Diaries and Intelligence Summaries are contained in F. S. Regs., Part II. and the Staff Manual respectively. Title pages will be prepared in manuscript.

Place	Date	Hour	Summary of Events and Information	Remarks and references to Appendices
AUCHEL	OCT 1		Visited section attached to 7 Bn. 2 Army. Laid down rd clay road lorries on paths when lorries in parks	W.O.C.
	2		Sent Serjt. Chappele to replace Corpl. Lyth with extra details section. Paid out Coy. Toft returned from M to SS just 1st Army. Visited ENQUIN LES MINES & arranged to continue as of cellar for storage at [found] per week.	W.O.C.
	3	11 a.m.	Toft kit inspection. Supply [Railheads] at LILLERS.	W.O.C.
	4		Men engaged in scavenging lost churches II section. No 1 section refitting tarpaulins.	W.O.C.
	5		Drew 2000 francs from field cashier	W.O.C.

WAR DIARY
or
INTELLIGENCE SUMMARY.
(Erase heading not required.)

Army Form C. 2118.

Place	Date	Hour	Summary of Events and Information	Remarks and references to Appendices
AUCHEL	Sept 6		H.Q and No 2 Section engaged in examining Boos Chambers	Ga
	7	11am	Route March. H.Q and No 2 Section completed examination of Boos Chambers. Sent for Saunders Car No 1812 to fit Zenith carburetter	Gu.
	8		Leave returns. 5 men today may be sent. Instructions received re care & conservation of Tube Material. Tyre press is now available at HAZEBROUCK. Instructions received to give all possible to supr Refineries & distilleries 30/c Brown of Vehicles has been withdrawn to Gen Hospl. Further NCO's have been detailed to Base MT Depot. See Extract from G.R.O of 1st July 1915. NCO's holding acting rank should revert to permanent rank prior to leaving their formations for the Base Depot.	9.9 28/2/38 CC 3774 DDγSγT 1st Army ST. 1671. DDSγT No ST 168.

Army Form C. 2118.

WAR DIARY
or
INTELLIGENCE SUMMARY.
(Erase heading not required.)

Instructions regarding War Diaries and Intelligence Summaries are contained in F. S. Regs., Part II. and the Staff Manual respectively. Title pages will be prepared in manuscript.

Place	Date	Hour	Summary of Events and Information	Remarks and references to Appendices
AUCHEL	9		Lt Campbell being one of officers in office work relieving of Sergeant in section.	acae 3 cd.
			Photos may be given to men who have not yet been sent. Monthly return of REC Officers should not be made out as required for the A.P.M.G., A.S.C. G.H.Q.	DDSST 1st army GM
"	10		Four men proceeded on leave.	
AUCHEL	11		Lt Hicks proceeded on leave of absence for 160 hrs.	
			Four men " " " " 72 "	
			French army ft orders proceedings on leave w/b exchanged at Victoria Station	copy cc 126/27
			Word was obtained from Zoer DENIEPPE in accordance with regulations laid down in 1st army Circular No 19.	1st army A 512/65.
			Received copies of traffic orders 1st army.	

1577 Wt. W10791/1773 500,000 1/15 D. D. & L. A.D.S.S./Forms/C. 2118.

Army Form C. 2118.

WAR DIARY
or
INTELLIGENCE SUMMARY.
(Erase heading not required.)

Instructions regarding War Diaries and Intelligence Summaries are contained in F. S. Regs., Part II. and the Staff Manual respectively. Title pages will be prepared in manuscript.

Place	Date	Hour	Summary of Events and Information	Remarks and references to Appendices
AUCHEL	12		Lieut Campbell to be Temporary Captain Aug 1st. 2/Lt Kirko " " " Lieutenant " "	G.R.O.
	13.		Received from 3rd 1st R. Berwicks the Stores Pair 6. N.I.V. 3620 &c.	C M No 100 G.R.
	14.		"Hypo" Helmets the withdrawn & "Tube" issued in their place.	G.R.
	15		Scale of winter clothing issued. Broken stone gravel are not to be removed from the roadways.	G.R.O. 1204. 1200

Army Form C. 2118.

WAR DIARY
or
INTELLIGENCE SUMMARY
(Erase heading not required.)

Instructions regarding War Diaries and Intelligence Summaries are contained in F. S. Regs., Part II. and the Staff Manual respectively. Title pages will be prepared in manuscript.

Hour, Date, Place	Summary of Events and Information	Remarks and references to Appendices
AUCHEL 17	Relieved 2000 sacks & rail head. Tool kit inspection. MT accountants to receive 6d a day additional pay.	A.G.Bone R.P. No 5400. E.f.m.
18th	Nil return of motor cycles & other abandoned cars in 6. A.D of Int. Car Corps. Men going on leave to receive a copy of regulations with their passes.	E.f.m.
19	Lt. White returned from leave. Jalouse in England. Packed on 20th at R.E.	

Army Form C. 2118.

WAR DIARY
or
INTELLIGENCE SUMMARY
(Erase heading not required.)

Instructions regarding War Diaries and Intelligence Summaries are contained in F. S. Regs., Part II. and the Staff Manual respectively. Title pages will be prepared in manuscript.

Hour, Date, Place	Summary of Events and Information	Remarks and references to Appendices
LAMBRES. 22nd	Moved here from AUCHEL arriving 4 p.m. Lt. Stewart with No 2 section rejoined Repark from the 7th Bde.	
23rd	Main road AIRE–LAMBRES not till much by motor lorries before 11.30 AM between 24th and 29th inclusive. Recovery of Cake filter caps on motor cycles.	S. of I. No 109.
24th	Lorry returned from collecting stores from 6th Bde & IOLC Stevens having taken 2½ days to complete. He wrote certified in need of repair. Rubber by no means necessarily for good running.	Grn

1247 W 3290 200,000 (E) 8/14 J.B.C. & A. Forms/C. 2118/11.

WAR DIARY
or
INTELLIGENCE SUMMARY

(Erase heading not required.)

Army Form C. 2118.

Instructions regarding War Diaries and Intelligence Summaries are contained in F.S. Regs., Part II. and the Staff Manual respectively. Title pages will be prepared in manuscript.

Hour, Date, Place	Summary of Events and Information	Remarks and references to Appendices
LAMBRES 25"	Arrangements were made for working in the Company. Took to look the materials for Lt. Cuming, later our driver 9°Clare 2nd CD.	CJn
26"	Ran jars & wooden cases the ushered Oils Supply Coc. for trans mission out Base.	CJn
27"	5 lorries required for Richards kestrels on 007 96. Po Bougon form ATC depts accumulator empty for Crew de abroad.	CJn

WAR DIARY
or
INTELLIGENCE SUMMARY.

Army Form C. 2118.

Place	Date	Hour	Summary of Events and Information	Remarks and references to Appendices
CAMBRES	27		Gear oil for back axels of Car boxes of motor cars and motor lorries	S & J CM No 110. CM.
			Demands for this at the Reft as tow as possible	
			Orders of Claim Commission c/o Cox's Bank	CM
			By Post c/o Boulogne Base	
	28		Ration issue made in the presence of an officer from this date.	CM
	29		Orders for lorries &c &c were received from OC 3rd Field Squadron	CM
			Green Leaves for Nos 1&cc received from ADM.	

Army Form C. 21

WAR DIARY
or
INTELLIGENCE SUMMARY.
(Erase heading not required.)

Place	Date	Hour	Summary of Events and Information	Remarks and references to Appendices
LAMBRES	30		R.O.D. Package 3/8 for Staves Commencing 1st Nov afternoon boat for Folkestone leaves Boulogne at 3 P.M.	
			H.Q. Lorries Nos: 4.5.6.7.8.9 proceeded to STRAZEELE & EBBLINGHEM for R.E. work.	gm.
	31		Lorries 4.5.6.7.8.9 HQ to STRAZEELE & EBBLINGHAM. Men under supervision of centurio the health in free rerun in every respect. Billeting in schools proven execpt in the fighting area	CC 1364/8
			List of ration & forage authorised scales	GRO Dis. 928. 235.
			Men ? & ? Pee to be sent here for testing as fitters re.	gm.
			J Marten Capt. ASC OC 2nd Cav Div. ? Park	

WAR DIARY or INTELLIGENCE SUMMARY

Army Form C. 2118

Place: AUCHEL
Date: October

Summary of Events and Information

Issues

No.	To whom issued	Nature	Remarks
149	4th Bde A.C.Bde	13pr HE	270
15	"	13pr Shrap.	
28,000	"	.303 S.A.	
720	6th Cav. Bde	Cartridges Very Pistol	
10,000	C. Middlesex	.303 S.A.	
60	1st Roy Dgns	Ball Grenades	
60	3rd Dgns Glds	"	
60	Somerset Yeo	"	
60	Roy 1st Glds	"	
60	10th Roy Hussars	"	
60	Essex Yeo	"	
108	1st Roy Dgns	"	
108	3 Dgm Glds	"	
108	Somerset Yeo	"	

Receipts

Date	No.	Received from	Nature
2.10.15	720	Laboury	Cartridges Very Pistol
8	2,000	"	Ball Grenades
"	36	A.O.D. M.G. Musk School	Hand Gre No 1
"	30	"	"
"	36	"	Tennis Grenade
"	40	"	Rifle Gre No 3
"	30	"	Chemical Gre
12	1692	Strazeele	Ball Grenades
18	12	O.O.O.S.	Mills Grenade
21	149	Laboury	13pr HE
"	15	"	13pr Shrap
2	28,000	"	.303 SA
3	10,000	"	.303 SA
14	14,000	"	.303 SA

Army Form C. 2118

WAR DIARY
or
INTELLIGENCE SUMMARY

(Erase heading not required.)

Instructions regarding War Diaries and Intelligence Summaries are contained in F. S. Regs., Part II. and the Staff Manual respectively. Title Pages will be prepared in manuscript.

Place	Date	Hour	Summary of Events and Information					Remarks and references to Appendices
			ISSUES.			Receipts		
			No.	To whom Issued	Nature	Remarks	Date	No. Received from Nature
AUCHEL	October							
	9		108	Roy Horse Gds	Ball. Grenades			
	"		108	10th Roy Hussars	"			
	"		108	Essex Yeo	"			
	"		36	H.Q. 8th Cav Bde	Mills Grenades			
	"		36	"	Hairite Gds			
	"		30	"	Hand Gds No 1			
	"		40	Roy Horse Gds	Rifle Gds No 3			
	"		40	"	Hand Gds No 2			
	"		30	"	Jamied Gds			
	25		200	10th Roy Hussars	Ball Grenades			
	"		6	"	Mills "			
	"		200	Roy H. Gds	Ball Grenades			
	"		6	"	Mills "			

WAR DIARY
or
INTELLIGENCE SUMMARY
(Erase heading not required.)

Army Form C. 2118

Place	Date	Hour	Summary of Events and Information			Remarks and references to Appendices
			ISSUES.			
			No	To whom issued	Nature	
AUCHEL	October 25		200	Essex Yeo	Ball. Grenade	Remarks on No. Recovered for Nature
			6	"	Mills	
			200	1st Life Guards	Ball. Grenade	
			6	"	Mills	
			200	2nd Life Guards	Ball. Grenade	
			6	"	Mills	
			200	Leicester Yeo	Ball. Grenade	
			6	"	Mills	
			600	3rd Dragoon Gds	Ball. Grenade	
			18	"	Mills	
	14		10,000	1st Life Gd. Col.	.303 S.A.	
			3,000	Essex Yeo	.303 S.A.	
	15		3,000	3rd D. Gds	.303 S.A.	

Army Form C. 2118

WAR DIARY
or
INTELLIGENCE SUMMARY
(Erase heading not required.)

Instructions regarding War Diaries and Intelligence Summaries are contained in F. S. Regs., Part II. and the Staff Manual respectively. Title Pages will be prepared in manuscript.

Place	Date	Hour	Summary of Events and Information	Remarks and references to Appendices
LAMBRES			ISSUES	
			No.	To whom issued	Nature	RECEIPTS Remarks	Date	No	Received from	Nature	
October	25		6,000	Somerset Yeo	·303 SA.						
	28		6,000	3rd Dgn Gds	·303 SA.						
	29										Chief Ordnance

1875 Wt. W593/826 1,000,000 4/15 J.B.C. & A. A.D.S.S./Forms/C. 2118.

3rd Cavalry Division

Confidential

War Diary
of
3rd Cavalry Ammunition Park.

From 1st Nov. 1915   To 30th Nov. 1915

(Volume 10.)

Army Form C. 2118

WAR DIARY
or
INTELLIGENCE SUMMARY.
(Erase heading not required.)

Instructions regarding War Diaries and Intelligence Summaries are contained in F. S. Regs., Part II. and the Staff Manual respectively. Title pages will be prepared in manuscript.

Place	Date	Hour	Summary of Events and Information	Remarks and references to Appendices
LAHBRE	Nov 1		Lorries Nos 456.789 HQ on R.T. WAR.	
	2		Inspected by Major Coulson ASC. Steering Rods & cross members behind Engine requiring attention.	D.R.O. 826.
	3		Command also ordered to overhaul for by roadway action.	C.K.
	4		Capt Campbell proceeded on leave of absence to England for 168 hrs.	A.D.C. 651
	5		Supplies of glycerine cannot be guaranteed	C.M
	6		A report to be sent in every motor vehicle taken in fournitures as to the want of an accident. Lorries not capable of taking 5 tons are shown as 30 cwt.	AD say 860/2

WAR DIARY
or
INTELLIGENCE SUMMARY.

(Erase heading not required.)

Army Form C. 2118

Place	Date	Hour	Summary of Events and Information	Remarks and references to Appendices
LAMBRES	Nov 6		Meeting has arranged with civil authorities. Reinforcements arriving on today are not to be included on A.F. B213 rendered on Saturday.	R.O. 833.
			One the penetrated in bulk of S.O's not by units.	S34
		7.	Left of two rollers shortened to advance. Four lorries over re-work.	S36

WAR DIARY
or
INTELLIGENCE SUMMARY.
(Erase heading not required.)

Army Form C. 211

Place	Date	Hour	Summary of Events and Information	Remarks and references to Appendices
LAMBTRES	Nov 8.		Unusual levies on R.E. Work. Divisional Com. call with O.C.a.r.	
	9		Deficiencies in each sheet of maps to be sent in monthly.	C/M
	10		6 Guns on R.E. work handed to HERECQUES. N.C.O's away proceeding on leave who will obtain an advanced course while in England air leave to produce evidence that Pay Books (A.B.64) other than those of the Com. contain work.	C/M DRO 545. C/M
	11		No 2 Section Army No 6 attached to Sugar Corps SILVESTRE.	C/M
	12		Capt. Campbell returned from leave. Cor. No 184 returned from O.C. R.O.C	

Army Form C. 2118

WAR DIARY
or
INTELLIGENCE SUMMARY.
(Erase heading not required.)

Instructions regarding War Diaries and Intelligence Summaries are contained in F. S. Regs., Part II. and the Staff Manual respectively. Title pages will be prepared in manuscript.

Place	Date	Hour	Summary of Events and Information	Remarks and references to Appendices
LINGRES	Nov 13		New regulations re Field Punishment. 6 Coxies to SERCUS.	
	14		6 Coxies to HEZECQUES. NCOs holding acting rank cannot to retain for long their N.C. of rank.	Yh
			Returns wanting as to new billets any claim should be investigated report forwarded to Div. Claim Office.	P.R.O. D.52
	15		Orders received to move STRUGES. 6 Coxies to HEZECQUES.	Yh
	16		moved STRUGES, ↓ Posts of billets.	Yh
	17		8 Coxies out- in Divisional area	

1577 Wt.W10791/1773 500,000 1/15 D.D. & L. A.D.S.S./Forms/C. 2118.

Army Form C. 2118

WAR DIARY
or
INTELLIGENCE SUMMARY.

(Erase heading not required.)

Instructions regarding War Diaries and Intelligence Summaries are contained in F. S. Regs., Part II. and the Staff Manual respectively. Title pages will be prepared in manuscript.

Place	Date	Hour	Summary of Events and Information	Remarks and references to Appendices
FRUGES	18		Leaving 6 lorries at SEAGULL with 3rd Fd. Sqdn.; for CALAIS. French differing material. Car is from OCATE for overhaul.	
	19		1 Officer & 20 men the centre a working party ATHE=CUREON. Obtained 40 tents complete from pulley stands from Station Det. Officio cookhouse house office to RUE SAINT OMER.	
	20		Lorry No 5. HQ Saint SILVESTRE believe Daimler lorry HQ.	
	21		Car No 1812 lent to No 6 Car Coy Dre whilst his own is under repair. A lorry to be sent from GHQ from time to time for overland Daily return or cars warrant is the daily embarkation from England.	1D Sgs. 875 SPO 872

1577 Wt. W10791/1773 500,000 1/15 D. D. & L. A.D.S.S./Forms/C. 2118.

WAR DIARY
or
INTELLIGENCE SUMMARY

Army Form C. 2118

Place	Date	Hour	Summary of Events and Information	Remarks and references to Appendices
FRUGES	Nov 22		6 lorries of No 1 Section sent to MARESQUEL for coal. Lorries not having arrived lorries returned & went to FERFAY & [?] with 12 tons coal.	
	23		20 men under Lieut Sturns wood cutting. 6 lorries of No 1 Section distributed coal to 6", 7 & 8" Brigades. 2 N.C.Os & men proceeding on leave to hear pt. of leave party en route. on A.S. 64	GRO 1267 W.T.C.
	24		20 men wood cutting. Marquess Fumio Tsin in severe using to expedience of Mrs Temp, 2 other Japanese. Capt Martin provided a 10 top lorry of stores to England. Address 31 Regules Rd, Chelsea	
	25		20 men wood cutting. Lieut Weller went to ABEELE to inspect lorries with standard section running to OUDEZONE Car No 1815 (British) with another car on return journey. Slight damage.	W.T.C.

WAR DIARY
or
INTELLIGENCE SUMMARY

Army Form C. 2118

(Erase heading not required.)

Place	Date	Hour	Summary of Events and Information	Remarks and references to Appendices
FRUGES	NOV 26		Held Court of Inquiry re loss of civy Lt Manzure. Court consisted of President Capt. McCaughill. Members Lieut. Kirk & A. Stevens. The Court found that this Offr was absent of accident. Sent 6 lorries to MARESQUEL to load for 7. B. S.	
	27		2 lt Luck left for 7 days leave of absence to England. 6 lorries delivered load to 7. B. S.	
	28		Sent 2 lorries to 7th Offrs to MARESQUEL from Brigade.	
	29		3 lorries to MARESQUEL to carry timber 7 " " FLECHINELLE for coal 1 " " BOMY to carry 8. B.S. S. 2 " " COYECQUE to carry hurs, chalets 1 " " CERCUS with rations & then on for wood from LAMOTTE	W.T.

Army Form C. 2118

WAR DIARY
or
INTELLIGENCE SUMMARY
(Erase heading not required.)

Place	Date	Hour	Summary of Events and Information	Remarks and references to Appendices
FROGES	NOV 30		2 lorries with coal to 8 B.9 I.	
			1 " " MARESQUEL to report to RE	
			5 " to DENNEBROEUC to move shelters for 10" Howitzers could not get over road to form house returned)	

WAR DIARY or INTELLIGENCE SUMMARY

Army Form C. 2118

(Erase heading not required.)

Instructions regarding War Diaries and Intelligence Summaries are contained in F. S. Regs., Part II. and the Staff Manual respectively. Title Pages will be prepared in manuscript.

Place	Date	Hour	Summary of Ammunition issued			Summary of Events and Information		Summary of Ammunition received		Remarks and references to Appendices
			No. of rounds	To whom issued	Nature of Ammn.	Date 1914	No. of rounds	Received from	Nature of Ammn.	
	Nov 1		15000	2" Life G.ds	.303 SA	2	25,000	STRAZEELE	.303 SA	
	5		8,000	1st S.G.	do	28	20,000	do	do	3
	11		1000	Cav. Life G.ds	do	"	1104	do	Pistol Webly	
	11		276	" "	Pistol Webly	"	1600	do	.303 SA	
	25		13000	10" Hussars	.303 SA	12	312	do	Mills bombs hd	
	25		276	" "	Pistol Webly	27	30	Essex Yeo	Woolwich Bomb	
	28		1104	3rd Cav. Ammn. Col	do	28	12	4th Bn 8th Aus. Col	Mills Grenades ho5	
	29		532	3" S.G.	do	29	48	do	do	
	24		156	10" Hussars	Bell Grenade	28	10	3rd Cav. Ammn. Col	Hand Grenades	
	26		40	6" Cav. Bs R.	Rifle do					
	"		40	7 " "	do do					
	"		40	8 " "	do do					
	"		24	6 " "	Mills Grenade					
	"		24	7 " "	do					
	"		24	8 " "	do					
	27		108	N. Somerset Yeo	Ball					
	"		204	3rd Cav. Ammn. Cars	do					
	"		90	10" Hussars	Vrennier smoke					
	"		108	N. Somerset Yeo	Bell Grenade					

Army Form C. 2118

WAR DIARY
or
INTELLIGENCE SUMMARY
(Erase heading not required.)

Place	Date	Hour	Summary of Ammunition Issued			Summary of Events and Information	Remarks and references to Appendices
			No of Rounds	To whom Issued		Nature of Ammunition	
	Nov						
	28"		24	3 Cav Ammun Coln		Mills Grenades No 5	
	28"		300	Railhead Stargale		Webbieds Bombs Complete	
	28"		8	do		Trench Mortars	
	28"		24	Leicesters 2/0		Mills Grenades No 5	
	29"		108	3 - S.S. Guards		Ball do	

W.O. Campbell
Capt ac
for O.C. 3 Cav Div Ammn - Park.

30-11-15.

Confidential
War Diary
of
3rd Cavalry Ammunition Park.
From 1st Dec. 1915 To 31st Dec. 1915.
(Volume H.)
XI

Army Form C. 2118

WAR DIARY
or
INTELLIGENCE SUMMARY
(Erase heading not required.)

Place	Date	Hour	Summary of Events and Information	Remarks and references to Appendices
FRUGES	Dec 1	7am	11 lorries to Railhead for R.E. work.	
		"	1 " to STRAZEELE for tools	
		5p.	Medical Inspection	
	2.	7am	19 lorries to Railhead for R.E. work	
		"	1 " to Strazeele for tools	
			Saw S.S.O. who said it was not necessary for lorries of lorries to load coal	
	3		7 lorries to Railhead for R.E. work	
			Saw future orders NCO's who must not draw advances of pay at Wimereux when on leave.	
		6p	Medical Inspection	

Army Form C. 2118

WAR DIARY
or
INTELLIGENCE SUMMARY
(Erase heading not required.)

Place	Date	Hour	Summary of Events and Information	Remarks and references to Appendices
FRUGES	Dec 4		A.D. of S. & T. inspected Park. Ordered men to be huts & men their accommodation. To be provided in billets.	
			2 lorries to Railhead for R.E. work	
	5		1 Coy with ammunition to 10th Hussars.	
			3 lorries to Railhead for R.E. work	
			1 " to St Sylvestre with fitter to repair lorry	A.S. of S.T. 906/15.
	6		2 " with B.303 S&A to Life Guards	
			Stores to the man to coor radiator when lorries have not been moved	
			2 S.T. Lorries proceeded to England on 7 days leave of absence.	
			6 lorries to Railhead for R.E. work.	WOR
	7		3 lorries to STRAZEELE for stores + R.E. work	

WAR DIARY
or
INTELLIGENCE SUMMARY
(Erase heading not required.)

Army Form C. 2118

Instructions regarding War Diaries and Intelligence Summaries are contained in F.S. Regs., Part II. and the Staff Manual respectively. Title Pages will be prepared in manuscript.

Place	Date	Hour	Summary of Events and Information	Remarks and references to Appendices
FRUGES	Dec 8		Establishment of S.A.A. to be carried attend to 318,000 rifle Ammn - i.e. 73.6 per rifle. 162,000 machine gun i.e. 4,500 per gun. 1800 mills 5 grenades. Capt Martin & 2nd Lieut RFA demitted to No 10 Officers Hospital	CC 3429
	9		Number of spare mules reduced from 50% to 25%. Mules to be sent up by untrained drivers. Ammn. Col returned 90,000 S.A.A. surplus Ammunition	
	10		2 lorries to MONTREUIL for R.E. work. Lorry with rations for EERCUS.	
	11.	3pm	Paid But Coy. Car to report to A.C.O i/c Post Office each evening at 3.50 p.m. Visited lorries at sheds & enquired them. Also found out the main items	O.C. ASC

Army Form C. 2118

WAR DIARY
or
INTELLIGENCE SUMMARY
(Erase heading not required.)

Instructions regarding War Diaries and Intelligence Summaries are contained in F.S. Regs., Part II. and the Staff Manual respectively. Title Pages will be prepared in manuscript.

Place	Date	Hour	Summary of Events and Information	Remarks and references to Appendices
FRUGES	Dec 12		Detailed lorry No 4 I Sect to return lorry with 73 Coy at ST SYLVESTRE	
	13		The 3 lorries to STRAZEELE with surplus S.A.A. & to draw rounds to complete 1800. Unable to draw other rounds.	
	14		Lorry with returns to section at SERGUS. Lorry to draw rounds for surplus S.A.A.	D.A.7 786G
	15		Generals stores only to issue to A.B M.T.D. rear BM.T.D. S&T	
			(1) Vehicles regiment action on return Lorries { Daimler { Bodin, Plaine st Denis, Paris. Albion OC 1st ASC Repair Shop, Rouencourt OC 3rd Arc. R. Shop. St Omer	
			Cap. Amtram Daniels (L) " " " "	

1875 Wt. W593/826 1,000,000 4/15 J.B.C. & A. A.D.S.S./Forms/C. 2118.

WAR DIARY
or
INTELLIGENCE SUMMARY

Army Form C. 2118

Place	Date	Hour	Summary of Events and Information	Remarks and references to Appendices
16 FRUGES	16		Attended aircraft hulls delivered to RA.	—
	17		Batts allotted to the unit from 17th sec. 16 men at a time from 4 – 5 daily.	—
	18		Demands for MT stores to be sent in on Sunday only. Officers during their certain roads may not be traversed by 3 ton lorries carrying hay wood see map.	D.O.T. Ch. No 122 ADRZ 399.
	19		SS Withern C qms Witham Sgt Chapple Dia Newnum reech confirmed in rank dated 21V.	

Army Form C. 2118

WAR DIARY
or
INTELLIGENCE SUMMARY
(Erase heading not required.)

Instructions regarding War Diaries and Intelligence Summaries are contained in F. S. Regs., Part II. and the Staff Manual respectively. Title Pages will be prepared in manuscript.

Place	Date	Hour	Summary of Events and Information	Remarks and references to Appendices
FRUGES	20		Have granted 3/a week on Thursdays. Smith coal wg. to purchase locally nos: have 6 ft. 2. 13/hr with bit off o/o forge vacancies.	C/lu
	21		Grenades d/o Ian "Bulls" returned to Railhead. Been to Enquin re battery fitters at work.	A.751. C/lu
	22		Stated 5 men future but found none suitable. Circular memorandum re Censorship re Green Envelopes posted on board.	C/lu
	23		Sub. Edwards to petrol each unit for certain journeys on a scale of 10% above.	3CD No 3306 /4
	24		Lorries returned from Leurs return from wounded.	
	25			

1875 Wt. W593/826 1,000,000 4/15 J.B.C. & A. A.D.S.S./Forms/C. 2118.

WAR DIARY
INTELLIGENCE SUMMARY
(Erase heading not required.)

Army Form C. 2118

Place	Date	Hour	Summary of Events and Information	Remarks and references to Appendices
FRUGES	26th		Personnel surplus wastage or casualties about to surrendered on B.A.C. Base	947 Ch. 123.
			Demands for Base Beaungo cancelled. Fresh demands to be received.	Copy Dep 7. 124.
			Check paid acting ranks with establishment	Org Section No 3987
"	27th		Acting ranks checked were surplus.	G/M
"	28th		Promotion of officers to be made as vacancies occur through the Corps & not in units	G/M Arc 977.
			2 Jan oil tins to be returned to No 3 Base Supply Depot.	G/M

WAR DIARY
or
INTELLIGENCE SUMMARY

(Erase heading not required.)

Army Form C. 2118

Instructions regarding War Diaries and Intelligence Summaries are contained in F. S. Regs., Part II. and the Staff Manual respectively. Title Pages will be prepared in manuscript.

Place	Date	Hour	Summary of Events and Information	Remarks and references to Appendices
FRUGES	29.		Received orders to proceed to BAPRIEUX on LILLERS-BETHUNE road on 1st Jan.	
"	30		Woodcutting at HESDIGUEL camp	
"	31		1 truck discharged from hospital, proceeded on leave. 6 n.c.m's proceeded to BAPRIEUX 19 lorries, 2 cars, 2 cycles	Charles Cox? Major R. O.C. 2 Coy?

WAR DIARY or INTELLIGENCE SUMMARY

(Erase heading not required.)

Army Form C. 2118

Instructions regarding War Diaries and Intelligence Summaries are contained in F.S. Regs., Part II. and the Staff Manual respectively. Title Pages will be prepared in manuscript.

Place	Date	Hour	Summary of Events and Information							Remarks and references to Appendices
			ISSUES				RECEIPTS			
			No.	To whom issued	Nature	Remarks	Date	No.	Received from	Nature
TRUCKS, Dec.										
	2		36,000	3rd Bgdn Gds	.303 S.A.A.					
	4		12,000	1st Roy. Dragoons	.303 S.A.A.		1	1008	Strazeele	Mills Grenades
	4		12,000	10th Roy. Hussars	.303 S.A.A.		7	1008	Strazeele	Ball Grenade
	4		1104	10th Roy. Hussars	Pistol Webley		21	1104	Strazeele	Pistol Webley
	6		32,000	1st Life Guards	.303 S.A.A.		21	7,212	Strazeele	Mills Grenades
	6		8,000	2nd Life Guards	.303 S.A.A.					
	7		4,000	10th Roy. Hussars	.303 S.A.A.					
	8		200	Essex Yeo.	Ball Grenade					
	8		200	1st Roy. Horse Gds.	Ball Grenade					
	8		200	6th Cav. Bde	Ball Grenade					
	8		300	6th Cav. Bde	Ball Grenade					
	9		844	6th Cav Bde	Mills Grenade					

WAR DIARY
or
INTELLIGENCE SUMMARY
(Erase heading not required.)

Army Form C. 2118

Place	Date	Hour	Summary of Events and Information	Remarks and references to Appendices
TRŨGIS. Dec.			ISSUES	

			No	To whom issued	Nature	Remarks	Date	No	Received from	Nature
	9		84	7th Cav Bde	Mills Grenades					
	9		84	8th Cav Bde	Mills Grenades					
	9		80	6th Cav Bde	Rifle Grenades					
	9		80	7th Cav Bde	Rifle Grenades					
	9		80	8th Cav Bde	Rifle Grenades					
	22		1060	6th Cav Bde	Mills Grenades					
	22		1026	7th Cav Bde	Mills Grenades					
	22		1056	8th Cav Bde	Mills Grenades					
	22		260	Am. Columns	Mills Grenades					
	26		240	1st Roy Dragoons	Cartridges Very Pistol					
	30		40	Leicester Yeo	Cartridges Very Pistol					

Lof C

Confidential
War Diary
of
3rd Cavalry Ammunition Park

From 1st January 1916 to 31st January 1916.

(Volume 12)

Army Form C. 2118

WAR DIARY
or
INTELLIGENCE SUMMARY
(Erase heading not required.)

Instructions regarding War Diaries and Intelligence Summaries are contained in F. S. Regs., Part II. and the Staff Manual respectively. Title Pages will be prepared in manuscript.

Place	Date	Hour	Summary of Events and Information	Remarks and references to Appendices
LE TAILLY	1st Jan 1916		Proceeded from TRUGES with 19 lorries reported DO & ISOff Parks. Workshop & HQ lorries left behind at AMN. Parks. Workshop & Lieut. Stewart.	GHn
"	2nd		FRUGES with Lt. Stewart. 6 lorries detailed for advance & RE work. Remainder to AUCHEL & reload. Build up road. SHA mobile workshop at FOUQUIERES S.E 21.a (Bethune cont) RE lorry reloaded here & then proceeded to VERMELLES to 3rd Fld Sqdn	
"	3rd		6 lorries detailed for Corn. Staff's work. Received Lt. ? returns regained.	GHn
"	4th		SAAP Office 30 BOULEVARDE FREDERIC GEORGE BETHUNE Arrange with car mob. sec. that lorries with artillery Pk. like at SSPK in FOUQUEREVIL.	GHn

1875 Wt. W593/826 1,000,000 4/15 J.B.C. & A. A.D.S.S./Forms/C. 2118.

Army Form C. 2118

WAR DIARY
or
INTELLIGENCE SUMMARY
(Erase heading not required.)

Place	Date	Hour	Summary of Events and Information	Remarks and references to Appendices
LE TOURET.	4.		6 bombers on advanced S.R.E. work.	R.O. 11.
			Units etc in possession of 2 smoke helmets	G/m.
			1 tony of PICKER for black	
			Estimated flow 11-1 × 6-8	
	5.		1 man stopped on leave on 9:45 13.45 20.45 24.45 31st train. 9.30 pm BETHUNE day type. Four loads of black from HUCHEL. 180 hand grenades nets No 5. RAP Section General scaffold not approved. Div HQ at SAILLY LA BOURSE	G/m

WAR DIARY
or
INTELLIGENCE SUMMARY

(Erase heading not required.)

Army Form C. 2118

Place	Date	Hour	Summary of Events and Information	Remarks and references to Appendices
LETALLY	6th		7 lorries BHQ & Division at SAILLY LABOURSE on arrival found Lorries are not required.	G.R.O. 1346
			R.A.M.C. 8th supplied with 1914 pattern Infantry Equipment.	G.R.O. 1347
			Motor cyclists detached Details 10th ROVEN the balance Relay Stop. DARNETAL near ROUEN	G/U
			On information the mobile on the Movement Order.	
"	7.		The 3 Cavalry Ammunition Parks reorganised on Disarmament on/Div Ord Parks Brigade Ammn Parks.	O.C. 1st 6th etc Parks.
			East Lancs Div ATT ting called a Brigade Ammn Parks.	
			Proposals O.C. 1st Corps Parks.	G/U
			On what ate sent on the 15th to D.A.D.C.	
"	8.		5 lorries to BETHUNE to carry stores.	
			1 lorry with hand grenades (fuse) reported the keys to RFA.	
			1 lorry attacked to OC 18th Corps Troops T.C.	G/U

WAR DIARY or INTELLIGENCE SUMMARY

Army Form C. 2118

Place	Date	Hour	Summary of Events and Information	Remarks and references to Appendices
LETAILLY	9.		4 lorries BTOUQUEREUIL with Ammunition for BAC. 4 lorries to L'ECLEME & then GAUCHEL start slag.; returned to L'ECLEME with working party. Bonnet covers of motor cars & motor lorries should be marked with the WD & number of the vehicle to which they belong. Size Cars 4" x 2½" lorries 6" x 5½"	BOT CM No 126.
"	10.		7 lorries to VERMELLES taking a working party from BETHUNE. Haggards & the men to workshops but only for stores. Should damage occur the officer responsible will have to find the money. 4 lorries to GONNEHEM to pick up working party returning GAUCHEL	BOT Circular Gen.
"	11.		7 lorries to SAILLY LABOURSE & pick up party returning to VERMELLES 2 lorries for grenades & SAA Ammunition to ear B? Corps.	Ggr

WAR DIARY
or
INTELLIGENCE SUMMARY

(Erase heading not required.)

Army Form C. 2118

Place	Date	Hour	Summary of Events and Information	Remarks and references to Appendices
LETAILLY	12		Attended lecture by APM 1st Corps on "Traffic Control".	C/M
			7 Lorries proceeded to BETHUNE to pick up working party taken there	
			OVER MELLE S	
			Section of Details Transport under Corpl for Censoring	
	13		7 Lorries proceeded to Cross Road ½ (NW) Vermelles returned with working party.	
			Ref RO 195 men proceeding on leave to be informed that if they are found with uncensored letters on them they will be placed	E.RO 612. 1357.
			under arrest and returned punit.	
			Local purchases of coal forbidden	C/M
			Cars to be overhauled every fortnight	ADMSS 958.
			Control posts for Cars to be formed. Office in Charge	CC 3788

Army Form C. 2118

WAR DIARY
or
INTELLIGENCE SUMMARY
(Erase heading not required.)

Instructions regarding War Diaries and Intelligence Summaries are contained in F. S. Regs., Part II. and the Staff Manual respectively. Title Pages will be prepared in manuscript.

Place	Date	Hour	Summary of Events and Information	Remarks and references to Appendices
LETAILLY	14.		Leave of Paris only granted by HQ of Army Corps.	DRO 994
			G H Q Order.	O.Cs.R. Returns. No 66.
			I G C.	
			Carrying away of Equipment & NCOs men from Battalions is forbidden	OD S & A No LY 12 p5-
			Another Spare parts for American Lorries & Cars to go to 2nd Base M T Depot- Calais	1 Jb/5 O/S
			Waistcoats awarded in lieu of shirts	14/162. 8 BM g I. Corps.
			Repairable Renewable servicewear stores serviceable leaded in the same case.	S J 1285.
			Charges against men by letter are to be brought before O C 1st Corps Ammn Parks.	Ellen

1875 Wt. W593/826 1,000,000 4/15 J.B.C. & A. A.D.S.S./Forms/C. 2118.

Army Form C. 2118

WAR DIARY
or
INTELLIGENCE SUMMARY
(Erase heading not required.)

Instructions regarding War Diaries and Intelligence Summaries are contained in F. S. Regs., Part II. and the Staff Manual respectively. Title Pages will be prepared in manuscript.

Place	Date	Hour	Summary of Events and Information	Remarks and references to Appendices
LETHEM	15		7 lorries to BETHUNE to collect working parties. Cross roads SW of VERMELLES.	GM
	16		7 lorries - do -	GM
			In future lorries are not to proceed further than VERMELLES without authority of 1st Corps. When waiting lorries are to return to BEUVRY.	GM
	17		7 lorries to cross road 1200x SW of VERMELLES. 1st Army Reserve Ammunition Train is at OA TREIZENNES 2 miles east of AIRE	GM
	18		7 lorries to VERMELLES. Forfeiture of Pay need not be written in when awarding Field Punishment.	GM

1875 Wt. W593/826 1,000,000 4/15 J.B.C. & A. A.D.S.S./Forms/C. 2118.

WAR DIARY
or
INTELLIGENCE SUMMARY

(Erase heading not required.)

Army Form C. 2118

Instructions regarding War Diaries and Intelligence Summaries are contained in F. S. Regs., Part II. and the Staff Manual respectively. Title Pages will be prepared in manuscript.

Place	Date	Hour	Summary of Events and Information	Remarks and references to Appendices
LETAILLY	19		6 Lorries out on fatigue work.	
"	20		13 x 18 pdr Blanket visors h/g covers the third first. Received Revised edition of Soldiers Pay Books ready for issue of opening a/c	SGD No 3608
"	21		Soldiers Pay Books ready for issue of opening a/c	920 1362
"	22		Acknowledgment demand of OC armoured MT cars clerc	DOT AM 1.30
"	23		4 Lorries on fatigue work.	

1875 Wt. W593/826 1,000,000 4/15 J.B.C. & A. A.D.S.S./Forms/C. 2118.

WAR DIARY
or
INTELLIGENCE SUMMARY
(Erase heading not required.)

Army Form C. 2118

Place	Date	Hour	Summary of Events and Information	Remarks and references to Appendices
LETAILLY	24		Jars to the taken that hand grenades to are not to be returned off park with details used in them.	10 Corps 139/75 Gen
"	25		Ca. No. 1813 received opens after our last at POGES	
"	26		When it is desired to hasten a long outstanding demand attention is emphised should be sent to DDSVS Gund 1. Date of demand 2. No " " 3. Description	HDSVS 826
		11pm	Three lorries with attached to wagon lines at LABOURSE. Two " A Ew loads & conveyed them to BHQ. FOUQUIERES	Gen
			Wire ropes and wire to lorry driver Brelfare worn out articles the unserviceable stores above to collected returned to HQ Park	Gen

1875 Wt. W593/826 1,000,000 4/15 J.B.C. & A. A.D.S.S./Forms/C. 2118.

WAR DIARY
or
INTELLIGENCE SUMMARY

(Erase heading not required.)

Army Form C. 2118

Place	Date	Hour	Summary of Events and Information	Remarks and references to Appendices
LETREXT	27		Motor Cycle Court generator sent out to was for lighting billets & home out outfitter work.	Sgt. Circular
"	28		No 13/10 ME with Gaine fuzes to be issued. Should store reflere in a demand.	Gen
	29		HEGamies I with 85/86 may be issued to RMC. Confidential memorandum re censorship. Operators not to allude to in private correspondence. GRO's 879, 1071 are cancelled. LO's with infants kirmonit Absentee Reports of men absent in UK to O/16 Records Reports of absentees in the country to APM.	Gen
	30		3 lorries to Vermelles with working party.	Gen

WAR DIARY
or
INTELLIGENCE SUMMARY

(Erase heading not required.)

Army Form C. 2118

Place	Date	Hour	Summary of Events and Information	Remarks and references to Appendices
LETAILLY	31.		The malleable iron hubs of the new wheels of 1.6/20 +.2 Wolseley Motor Cars & Ambulances having proved too weak the Company have brought out a new pattern of hub steel with a detachable centre + of stronger material.	Sgt E.M. 31
			Tools & Equipment of cars should be checked at fortnightly review	WDSr1/9 958/1/6. page 1084
			Cars of Personnel to be reported to Car. Coy. Little Circ. "Leaves" should always be shown as "fully details"	Car Circ No 4

WAR DIARY
or
INTELLIGENCE SUMMARY
(Erase heading not required.)

Army Form C. 2118

Place	Date	Hour	Summary of Events and Information	Remarks and references to Appendices
LETAILLY	5		Ammunition supplied received	
	6		282 rounds 13th HE from 4th Bde RHA AC at ESTREE BLANCHE	
			2160 mills Hand Grenades No 5 to 4th Bde " "	
			396 hills Hand Grenades " " " at FOUQUIÈRES	
			3720 Very Lights 1" " " " "	
			60 Rifle Grenades No 3 " " "	
	9		1016 Rds Shrapnel from Ox Hair LAPUGNOY (Raillent)	
			1016 " to 4th Bde AC	
	10		664 Rds Shrapnel 13td from LAPUGNOY	
			816 " " to 4th Bde AC.	
	11		1200 V Lights issued to 4th Bde AC	

WAR DIARY
or
INTELLIGENCE SUMMARY

Army Form C. 2118

Place	Date	Hour	Summary of Events and Information	Remarks and references to Appendices
LETAILLY	12	1656	Rds Webley Pistol issued to 1st Corps Bomb Sch.	
		720	Very Lights " " " "	
		320	Rds 18½" Shrapnel from Ox Train	
		448	" " " to A.C.	
"	13	144	Rds 18½" Shrapnel from Ox	
			" " to 16 A C	
"	14	50	Rds 1½" TM Heavy Mk II from 1st Corps Bomb Sch	
		50	" " " " to 16 A C	
		936	" 18½" Shrapnel from Ox	
			" " " to 16 A C	
"	15	50	Rds 2" TM Ammunition with 314 Fuze from 1st Corps Bomb Sch	
		50	" " " " to 16 A C	
		50	" 1½" TM Heavy Amm: Mk II from Bomb Sch	
		50	" " " " to 16 A C	

Army Form C. 2118

WAR DIARY
or
INTELLIGENCE SUMMARY
(Erase heading not required.)

Instructions regarding War Diaries and Intelligence Summaries are contained in F.S. Regs., Part II. and the Staff Manual respectively. Title Pages will be prepared in manuscript.

Place	Date	Hour	Summary of Events and Information	Remarks and references to Appendices
LETAILLY	15		608 Rds 13hr Shrapnel from Ox to A.C.	
			608 " " " " "	
"	16		100 Rds 4hr TM Ammn from Bomb Wks to A.C.	
			100 " " " " "	
			388 " 13hr Shrapnel from Ox to A.C.	
			388 " " " " "	
"	17		2760 Rds Pistol Webley from Ox to A.C.	
			456 " 13hr Shrapnel from Ox to A.C.	
			456 " " " " "	
"	18		2760 Rds Pistol Webley to A.C.	
			380 Rds 13hr Shrapnel from Ox to A.C.	
			380 " " " " "	
			8000 "SAA" from Ox to A.C.	
			8000 " " " "	

Army Form C. 2118

WAR DIARY
or
INTELLIGENCE SUMMARY
(Erase heading not required.)

Instructions regarding War Diaries and Intelligence Summaries are contained in F. S. Regs., Part II. and the Staff Manual respectively. Title Pages will be prepared in manuscript.

Place	Date	Hour	Summary of Events and Information	Remarks and references to Appendices
LETAILLY	19		5.32 Rdo 13th Shrapnel from OX to AC. 5.32 " " " " " "	
"	20		6.08 Rdo 13th Shrapnel from OX to AC 6.08 " " " " " " 29,000 Rdo SAA from OX 2nd Bn Ann Park 14,000 " " " " " 43,000 " " " " to AC.	
"	21		5.24 Rdo 13th Shrapnel from OX to AC. 5.24 " " " " "	
"	22		4.80 Very lights white 1" from Bond Ste 4.80 " " " " " 15 AC 1.04 Cartridges illuminating 1½"DI from Bond Str 1.04 " " " " 15 AC 304 Rdo 13th Shrapnel from OX 304 " " " " 15 AC.	

WAR DIARY
or
INTELLIGENCE SUMMARY

(Erase heading not required.)

Army Form C. 2118

Place	Date	Hour	Summary of Events and Information	Remarks and references to Appendices
LETAILLY	23		50 2" TM Bombs with 31A fuze from Bomb Sch 50 " " " " " " to A C 64 1½" TM Bombs Heavy MK II from Bomb Sch 64 " " " " " " to A C 16 1½" TM Bombs Heavy MK I from Bomb Sch 16 " " " " " " to A C 100 Detonator Rifle Grenades No 3 from Bomb Sch 100 " " " " " to A C 1100 Rds Ammn piercing Mark VII from O X 1100 " " " " " to A C 192 Rds '3 hr shrapnel from O X 192 " " " " to A C	
	24		20 Rockets Green from Bomb Sch 20 " " to A C	

WAR DIARY
or
INTELLIGENCE SUMMARY
(Erase heading not required.)

Army Form C. 2118

Place	Date	Hour	Summary of Events and Information	Remarks and references to Appendices
LETAIUY	26		824 Rds 13 Pr Shrapnel from Ox	
"	27		75 Rds 1½" TM Light Amm: MkII from Bone Shed to AC	
			75 " " " " " "	
			200 Rds 4 pr TM Amm: from Bone Shed to AC	
			200 " " " " " "	
			50,000 Rds SAA from Ox to AC	
			50,000 " " " " "	
			972 Rds 13 Pr from Ox to "C" Battery RHA	
			624 " " " 13 " "	
			488 " " " " "	
			684 " " " 9 " "	

Army Form C. 2118

WAR DIARY
or
INTELLIGENCE SUMMARY
(Erase heading not required.)

Instructions regarding War Diaries and Intelligence Summaries are contained in F. S. Regs., Part II. and the Staff Manual respectively. Title Pages will be prepared in manuscript.

Place	Date	Hour	Summary of Events and Information	Remarks and references to Appendices
LESTREM	28		153 Rds 13th Shrapnel to G Battery RHA	
			148 " " " " "	
			300 " " " from O.K.	
			50 Newton Rifle Grenade from Bomb Shed	
			50 " " to AC	
			16 Percussion Primers N.I from Bomb Shed	
			16 " " to AC	

WAR DIARY
or
INTELLIGENCE SUMMARY

(Erase heading not required.)

Army Form C. 2118

Place	Date	Hour	Summary of Events and Information	Remarks and references to Appendices
LE TOUQUET	29		688 Rds Shrapnel from Ox Train to "G" Battery RHA	
			152 " " " " " 12 " " "	
			136 " " " " " " "	
			400 " " " " to A C	
			128 Rds of 4.4 HE 13 hr from Railhead St VENANT ⎫ Issued	
			80/85 " " " " " ⎬ to	
			12 " " genie I " " " ⎭ A C	
			500 Rifle Grenades from Bond Shed to Bond Shed	
			500 " " " " "	
			100 " " " No 3 from 1st Corps Bond Shed	
			100 " " " " " to A C	
			160 Detonators for New Gun Rifle Grenades from Bond Shed to A C	
			85 Portfires from Bond Shed to A C	
			85 " " " "	
			500 Rifle Grenades from Guards Div in Art Park St VENANT 1st Corps Bond Shed	GW
			500	

WAR DIARY
or
INTELLIGENCE SUMMARY

Army Form C. 2118

Place	Date	Hour	Summary of Events and Information	Remarks and references to Appendices
ISTAMBUL	30		268 Rds 13 pr. Shrapnel from OX to AC	Sgn
"	31		268 " " " " "	
			200 Cartridges for Rifle Grenades from Bomb Store to AC	
			200 " " "	

Army Form C. 2118

WAR DIARY
or
INTELLIGENCE SUMMARY
(Erase heading not required.)

Mileage reported Brompton for January:

	Miles	Galls.	Miles per Gallon
Heavy Section	2358	388	6.08
First "	4946	814	6.07
Second "	3500	578	6.05
Workshops		104	
Total Lorries	10,804	1780	6.07
" Cars	1,338	85	15.62
" Cycles	4,338	101	42.95

J.M.

Lot C

Confidential
War Diary
of
3rd Cavalry Ammunition Park.

From 1st Feb. 1916   To 29 Feb. 1916

(Volume 13.)

Army Form C. 2118

WAR DIARY
or
INTELLIGENCE SUMMARY
(Erase heading not required.)

Place	Date	Hour	Summary of Events and Information	Remarks and references to Appendices
LE TALLY	1		Magnetos for repair should be returned to Base MT Depot v DGTS Circular No 117	ADS v8 934/1
			Lorries HE charged for 85 type over Genie I 3 Lorries OVERMELLES with party of Div: Div:	CH
	2		Arrangements are to be made to notify change the RA personnel in the Conurbation Parks with those in the more forward Echelons also to be taken to ensure that arrangements are given railway warrants Before acting appointments are made to complete establishments reference must be made the OC Base MT Depot.	1st Corps No 5490 ASC Section 38887
			Salvaging getting slack 3 Lorries OVERMELLES with party of Div: Div:	APO 271
	3		3 Lorries Vermelles with working party when slags or supplies are issued or received from French military authorities a record will be kept. 3/7 for 5 tres.	RE 1083

WAR DIARY
or
INTELLIGENCE SUMMARY
(Erase heading not required.)

Army Form C. 2118

Place	Date	Hour	Summary of Events and Information	Remarks and references to Appendices
LETAILLY	4th		3 Lorries AVELUY with working party of dismounted Division Demands for R.E. Personnel	DOT CM 133
			1 Ordinary Demand on B.213A Reynolds Slip	
			2 " " by letter or telegram	
			3 Urgent demand – not met - will be made on report of A.F.B.213A	Glm
"	5		3 Lorries OVERVILLERS with working party	Glm
"	6		An AAA of "N" manufacture to be returned deflected. Splinter of the same with signs of extraction from the rifle	1st Corps 5013/36
			3 Lorries OVERVILLERS with working party	Glm

WAR DIARY
or
INTELLIGENCE SUMMARY

(Erase heading not required.)

Army Form C. 2118

Place	Date	Hour	Summary of Events and Information	Remarks and references to Appendices
LATTRUY	7		(1) A private holding the acting rank of Sergt. may be reverted by his C.O. to the acting rank of Corporal or to the ranks. (11) A Corporal holding the acting rank of C.Q.M.S. may be reverted to acting Sergt. or to Corporal	G.R.O. 1388
			3 Lorries to Vermelles with working party made two journeys	G.R.
	8		Three lorries on. Two to VERMELLES & SOUTREZON YARD.	G.R.O. 986.
	9		Horses must not be tied up to limbers, wagons or other vehicles. Purchase of Supplies in the field will be carried out by A.S.C. Requisition 9327. Officers when Corps is at rest	G.R.
	10		Bonnet covers completed & handing of numbers dashboards started. A dim could that no lorries are be taken by officers when neuf barrel to place if forces for 1st & 2nd Drivers from Cavel Contents.	G.R.

WAR DIARY
or
INTELLIGENCE SUMMARY

(Erase heading not required.)

Army Form C. 2118

Place	Date	Hour	Summary of Events and Information	Remarks and references to Appendices
LETALLY	11		W.O's, NCO's, men & ASC serving in regular Army Engagements are ineligible for Commissions	A2C 1104
"	12		Campaign Comfort Gloves distributed amongst Drivers	Glen
"	13		Three lorries out/shop for repair work. Capt Campbell went on leave of absence in England: returns on 22nd of the month. Permission for officers stationed on leave being given in leaves outside the Brital office the distance from Hd. of Bn.	DRO 993
"	14		—	

WAR DIARY
or
INTELLIGENCE SUMMARY

(Erase heading not required.)

Army Form C. 2118

Place	Date	Hour	Summary of Events and Information	Remarks and references to Appendices
LETAIGNY	15		A new type of rear slung bucket for Dunkan Cars changed, details to	Sof's C.M. No 135-
"			be placed on Adv. M.T.D.	C.M. No 136.
			Spareparts demanded for a vehicle which is subsequently evacuated	
			will be taken	
	16		O.C.'s Divisional Sanitary sqd & O.C. Boys of Coys & Divisional will	G.R.O. 1408.
			notify O.C. Coy of lorries must (1) when soldier is sent to hospital the Coy from	
			a Field Ambulance or Casualty Clearing Station	
			(11) when him transferred	
			when soldier admitted goes to hospital / invalid must be placed	G.R.O. 1411
			in between Dufaux Stretcher pieces	

WAR DIARY
or
INTELLIGENCE SUMMARY

(Erase heading not required.)

Army Form C. 2118

Place	Date	Hour	Summary of Events and Information	Remarks and references to Appendices
LE TAILLY	17		Gas supply. When local production made by units AT W.3315 could be used	SPO 997.
			3.7" Howitzer ground "Grenade ML 3.J." To H3r "not found"	998
			Lee GPO 1156. re improper Chemical Trators &c	1002
			On 29th drew from Valona at 9.15 p.m.	[sig]
"	18		Action taken when motor vehicle are damaged by fire or gunfire	D/17 9726
"	19		grew 1800 hills Landriencer complete establishment	
"	20	11 AM	Car 1815 Sunbeam return accident in collision with french Sunbeam badly wrecked. Car No: 6780.	
FRUGES	22		Returned with 1&2 Rectors from LE TAILLY.	

WAR DIARY
or
INTELLIGENCE SUMMARY
(Erase heading not required.)

Army Form C. 2118

Place	Date	Hour	Summary of Events and Information	Remarks and references to Appendices
FRUGES	22nd		Candidates for Commissions whose names appear in the weekly list of Appointments, Promotions &c will be Gazetted as officers immediately.	GRO 14/3
			Rate of exchange 27.90 frcs to the £1	14/17
	23rd		Capt Campbell returned from leave of absence in England.	
	24		Capt Martin proceeded on leave of absence to England returning on 4-3-16. 8 Lorries to STRAZEELE for S.A.A. 2½ tons in charge Lieutenant about 9.30p & reported road in very bad condition.	
	25		All leave stopped. Those at present on leave will not be recalled. 4 Lorries to ABEELE with 13 P.R. Shrapnel. Returned 10.45pm. Lieut in charge reported roads deep in snow	10/c

Army Form C. 2118

WAR DIARY
or
INTELLIGENCE SUMMARY
(Erase heading not required.)

Instructions regarding War Diaries and Intelligence Summaries are contained in F. S. Regs., Part II. and the Staff Manual respectively. Title Pages will be prepared in manuscript.

Place	Date Feby	Hour	Summary of Events and Information	Remarks and references to Appendices
FRUGES	26	12.30p	Test Kit inspection. Inspected Billets	
		12.45	2 lorries to collect 13 P.R. from Aires	
	27		Heavy snow & frost all day. Told Kit inspection.	
	28	12.30p	Medical Inspection 2/t Stevens with 15 men to billets at HEZECQUE for mtr) arty.	
	29	12.30p	Lorry took 3 vehicles to T ISBERG for & returning. Rifle inspection.	WOC

W.O. Campbell Capt
For O.C 3 Res Aux Park

WAR DIARY
or
INTELLIGENCE SUMMARY

(Erase heading not required.)

Army Form C. 2118

Instructions regarding War Diaries and Intelligence Summaries are contained in F. S. Regs., Part II. and the Staff Manual respectively. Title Pages will be prepared in manuscript.

Place	Date	Hour	Summary of Events and Information							Remarks and references to Appendices
			ISSUES			RECEIPTS				
			No	To Whom Issued	Nature	Date	No	Received from	Nature	
FRUGES										
February	10		828	Regimental Hd.	Pistol Webley	2nd	1104	Skagedal	Pistol Webley	
	19		12,000	1st Rgt 65pnr	.303 S.A.A.	18th	100,000	—	.303 S.A.A.	
	"		1104	—	Pistol Webley	"	2,208	—	Pistol Webley	
	"		828	3rd Dgns Gds	Pistol Webley	24	40,000	—	.303 S.A.A.	
	"		6,000	N Som Yeo	.303 S.A.A.	"	3,312	—	Pistol Webley	
	"		6,000	10th Ry Hussars	.303 S.A.A.					
	"		1932	"	Pistol Webley					
	"		27,000	Regimental Gds	.303 S.A.A.					
	"		12,000	Essex Yeo	.303 S.A.A.					
	"		552	Leicester Yeo	Pistol Webley					
	23		42,500	1st Ry Dgns	.303 S.A.A.					
	"		44,000	3rd Dgn Gds	.303 S.A.A.					
	"		60,000	Somerset Yeo	.303 S.A.A.					
	"		40,000	1st Life Gds	.303 S.A.A.					

WAR DIARY
or
INTELLIGENCE SUMMARY
(Erase heading not required.)

Army Form C. 2118

Place	Date	Hour	Summary of Events and Information		Remarks and references to Appendices
FRUGES			ISSUES		
February			No. To whom issued	Nature	
	23		16,000 2nd Life Guards	303 SAA	
	"		29,000 Leicester Yeo	303 SAA	
	"		63,000 Roy Horse Gds	303 SAA	
	"		34,000 1st Roy Dragoons	303 SAA	
	"		103,000 Essex Yeo	303 SAA	
	"		6,000 Somerset Yeo	303 SAA	
	24		20,000 2nd Life Gds	303 SAA	
	"		2,000 1st Roy Dragoons	303 SAA	
	25		972 "A BEELE"	13th Sngrs	

Confidential
War Diary
of
3rd Cavalry Ammunition Park.
From 1st March 1916 to 31st March 1916.
(Volume 14)

Army Form C. 2118

WAR DIARY
or
INTELLIGENCE SUMMARY
(Erase heading not required.)

Instructions regarding War Diaries and Intelligence Summaries are contained in F. S. Regs., Part II. and the Staff Manual respectively. Title Pages will be prepared in manuscript.

Place	Date	Hour	Summary of Events and Information	Remarks and references to Appendices
FRUGES	March 1		Sewbram Car No 1815 sent to GHQ as unserviceable & asked for new car, to replace.	
	2.		Inspected HUMBERSENT for billets etc. Found very small accommodation for lorries workshops.	
			Received orders to evacuate to Base 8 employees lorries. There is new from 2 Coy M.T. men as historian etc.	
	3.		Evacuated 8 employees lorries to Base.	
			Received orders that the Division will not move.	
	4.		Our Cars to Cavalry Corps HQ for 2 Hotchkiss guns	
			Heavy snow all this morning.	
	5.	12.	Obtained 54000 S.A.A to be carried by Park making 534.000 S.A.A.	
			Kept Inspecting HUCQUELIERS with R.E. Stores	WMC
			2 lorries to HUCQUELIERS with R.E Stores	
			8 men sent to Div S.O for Fatigues	

Army Form C. 2118

WAR DIARY
or
INTELLIGENCE SUMMARY
(Erase heading not required.)

Instructions regarding War Diaries and Intelligence Summaries are contained in F.S. Regs., Part II. and the Staff Manual respectively. Title Pages will be prepared in manuscript.

Place	Date	Hour	Summary of Events and Information	Remarks and references to Appendices
FRUGES	MARCH 5		Owing to Epidemic of Measles at FLEETWOOD men are not to go from here to that place.	
	6.	12.0	Got kit inspection & inspection of billets. 2 Lorries to STRAZEELE for S.A.A. & bomb.	
	7		1 Lorry to Amm: Col. to pick up Officers that were taking them to WESTERHAM. 2 Lorries to Reg. amnts. for Instruction of ammunition. 1 to station for stores. 1 to 3 Field Squadron for R.E. work. Heavy snow in afternoon evening.	
	8		Heavy snow all night lying 2 feet thick. Orders for details of lorries cancelled on account of snow. M.S.S.M. Stock taking in store lorry. Captain Martin has returned to 12-3-16.	W.O.C

WAR DIARY or INTELLIGENCE SUMMARY

Army Form C. 2118

Place	Date	Hour	Summary of Events and Information	Remarks and references to Appendices
Lurgan	March 9		1. Lorry to collect Hotchkiss fittings from S.A.S.O.C. & take them to 8th Bn. Also Lorry also to take 4 Hotchkiss guns to 6.7.& 8. Bns.	
			1 Lorry to LA MOTTE (for wood).	
			4 Lorries to WARDRECQUES for stores.	
			2 Lorries to STRAZEELE for S.A.A.	
			Rifle inspection.	
	10	2 p.	Recend order to send 1 Pte (Kemshed, Taylor & Stamford) to Havre as fillers.	
	11		2 Lorries to HUMBERT with stores.	
		12 a.	Kit inspection	
		12.30	Billet Inspection.	

W.M.C.

Army Form C. 2118

WAR DIARY
or
INTELLIGENCE SUMMARY
(Erase heading not required.)

Instructions regarding War Diaries and Intelligence Summaries are contained in F.S. Regs., Part II. and the Staff Manual respectively. Title Pages will be prepared in manuscript.

Place	Date	Hour	Summary of Events and Information	Remarks and references to Appendices
FRUGES	MARCH			
	12	12.2	Took kit inspection. In future all returns for DADS+T, GHQ to go through O.C. A.S.C. In future when transferring vehicles an equipment report to is sent with them. Also when receiving which an equipment report to be completed.	See S.I. S+T. GHQ
			Capt Martin returned from leave. List of returns received from O came rendered by DADO/S+T GHQ. Returns to be rendered to office of OC A.S.C.	3 ED. AOC 1185
	13		Inoculation with new serum against typhoid. 38 names given in.	
	14		Postal orders may be obtained from an FPO. French note may not be sent through the post.	

1875 Wt. W593/826 1,000,000 4/15 J.B.C. & A. A.D.S.S./Forms/C. 2118.

WAR DIARY
or
INTELLIGENCE SUMMARY

Army Form C. 2118

Place	Date	Hour	Summary of Events and Information	Remarks and references to Appendices
FRUGES	14		Motorcars sparking plugs should be returned before new ones are issued.	JM
	15		Motor Cyclist Handle Bars not to be bent. Chaps against their being in future undergo its fortnightly cancellation	DRO 1048. JM
			Lewbram Car No M 15373 will in future undergo its fortnightly inspection in the workshop.	
	16		Claim for 25 steel coil drum is now forwarded to followers. Received copies of map Palais 13. Reference in future will be made to [Steels]	JM
	17		Two lorries attached from GHQ for carrying supplies etc Qr. Labour Battalion	JM
	18		Baines Car now doing 16 miles to the gallon after adjusting	JM

WAR DIARY or INTELLIGENCE SUMMARY

Army Form C. 2118

Place	Date	Hour	Summary of Events and Information	Remarks and references to Appendices
RUCES	20		Correspondence circulation of funds	
			Annex in words of First Army	G.R.O. 1459.
			Corps. Donn. appn. of II Corps.	
			Divisions &c in Arabic figures eg. 3rd Div:	
	21		Billeting Certificate. Difficult observed to O/i/c Branch	G.R.
			Regn. shown Office. G.H.Q.	
			N2 G. 1098 431 reveal available to be Army Rents	G.R.
	22		Lt Rushe recommended for Capt. L.S.	
			2d Sirens	

Army Form C. 2118

WAR DIARY
or
INTELLIGENCE SUMMARY
(Erase heading not required.)

Place	Date	Hour	Summary of Events and Information	Remarks and references to Appendices
FRUGES	23		Daimler Lorry 36on Type CD WD No. G591 transferred to 3rd Cav: Supply Col: 1st Driver McStrode. 2nd Driver McLeod.	C/M.
"	24		Lorries of Amm: Parks not the march for general transport work divisional Area.	Acc 1197.
"	25		Liables claims by inhabitants. Report made out.	
"	26		Increase of green curtilages to be promulgated. Ammunition Parks. Inter La Di Ad Qr for moves 2. Northern STAFF.	GRO. 1470
			Ammunition Park check took with Amm: Col:	1472.

Army Form C. 2118

WAR DIARY
or
INTELLIGENCE SUMMARY
(Erase heading not required.)

Instructions regarding War Diaries and Intelligence Summaries are contained in F. S. Regs., Part II. and the Staff Manual respectively. Title Pages will be prepared in manuscript.

Place	Date	Hour	Summary of Events and Information	Remarks and references to Appendices
ROUEN	27		Packing cases of stores returned from Base should not be utilized for fire wood.	Cfm/145
"	28		Re-enlisted men's Records shewed against unit. Base Officers whereabouts on leave in settled locations. Departure.	146 BRO 1065
"	29		Accident between Car No 15805 & Lorry No. 8 Sec. 2. No 17679. Two officers in car hurt whilst vehicles damaged.	Cfm
"	30		Supervision of demands for spare parts, tools &c. for MT vehicles. Copy taken.	Cfm/Cor
"	31		On rejt/G 30th Divn: No officers or other ranks are allowed to salute MONTREUIL without a pass. One reinforcement arrived from Base.	BRO 1067. Cfm/Marti Coln 3rd Cav Divn Park. Oc Cfm 1/6.

1875. Wt. W593/826 1,000,000 4/15 J.B.C. & A. A.D.S.S./Forms/C. 2118.

Army Form C. 2118

WAR DIARY
or
INTELLIGENCE SUMMARY
(Erase heading not required.)

Instructions regarding War Diaries and Intelligence Summaries are contained in F. S. Regs., Part II. and the Staff Manual respectively. Title Pages will be prepared in manuscript.

Place	Date	Hour	Summary of Events and Information							Remarks and references to Appendices
			ISSUES			RECEIPTS				
			No	To whom issued	Nature	Date	No	Received from	Nature	
FRUGES										
March	1		1,000	3rd Field Amb RE	.303 SAA	March 6th	1104	Chingale	Pistol Webley	
	"		276	3rd Field "	Pistol Webley	"	92,000	—	.303 S.A.A.	
	5		26,000	Leicester Yeo	.303 S.A.A.	" 9	168,000	—	.303 S.A.A	
	7		10,000	Essex Yeo	.303 SAA	" 25	42,000	—	.303 S.A.A	
	"		828	Essex Yeo	Pistol Webley	"	1656	—	Pistol Webley	
	"		24,000	10th Roy Hussars	.303 S.A.A.	" 29	60,000	—	.303 S.A.A	
	"		26,000	Roy Horse Guards	.303 S.A.A.	" 19	2,508	Capt Mr Park	Mills GRENADES	
	"		49,000	1st Life Gds	.303 SAA	"	1500	"	Bell Grenade	
	"		276	2nd Life Gds	Pistol Webley	" 21	300	34th Division	Bell Guards	
	"		26,000	1st Life Gds	.303 SAA					
	"		25,000	1st Roy Sqdn	.303 SAA					
	"		336	6th Cav Bde	Mills GRENADES					
	"		336	7th Cav Bde	Mills GRENADES					
	"		336	8th Cav Bde	Mills GRENADES					

Army Form C. 2118

WAR DIARY
or
INTELLIGENCE SUMMARY
(Erase heading not required.)

Instructions regarding War Diaries and Intelligence Summaries are contained in F.S. Regs., Part II. and the Staff Manual respectively. Title Pages will be prepared in manuscript.

Place	Date	Hour	Summary of Events and Information		Remarks and references to Appendices
FRUGES	March		ISSUES		
			No	To whom issued	Nature
	9		14,000	6th Machine Gun Sqn	.303 SAA
	10		12,000	10th Roy. Hussars	.303 SAA
	"		4,000	Leicester Yeo	.303 SAA
	12		552	1st Life Gds	Pistol Webley
	13		2,000	2nd Roy. Dragoons	.303 SAA
	18		3,000	Divisional Cav. Regt	.303 SAA
	"		1,608	"	Mills Grenades
	"		1,500	"	Ball Grenades
	19		300	6th Cav. Bde	Mills Grenades
	19		300	7th Cav. Bde	Mills Grenades
	"		300	8th Cav. Bde	Mills Grenades
	23		11,000	6th Cav. Bde	.303 SAA
	"		3,000	6th M.G. Sqn	.303 SAA
	27		14,000	10th Roy. Hussars	.303 SAA
	"		14,000	Roy. Horse Gds	.303 SAA

WAR DIARY or INTELLIGENCE SUMMARY

Army Form C. 2118

Place	Date	Hour	Summary of Events and Information		Remarks and references to Appendices
			ISSUES		
			No / To whom issued	Nature	
FRUGES	March 27		14,000 Essex Yeo	.303 SAA	
	"		11,000 1st Cav Bde	.303 SAA	
	"		10,000 1st Life Gds	.303 SAA	
	"		10,000 2nd Life Gds	.303 SAA	
	"		10,000 Leicester Yeo	.303 SAA	
	"		10,000 1st Roy Dragoons	.303 SAA	
	"		10,000 3rd Dgn Gds	.303 SAA	
	"		10,000 Somerset Yeo	.303 SAA	
	"		6,000 6th M.G. Section	.303 SAA	
	"		276 1st Bde R.H.A.	Pistol Webley	

L of C

Confidential
War Diary
-of-
3rd Wadaloey Ammunition Park.

From 1st April 1916   T.o 30th April 1916

(Volume 15)

Army Form C. 2118

WAR DIARY
or
INTELLIGENCE SUMMARY
(Erase heading not required.)

Instructions regarding War Diaries and Intelligence Summaries are contained in F.S. Regs., Part II. and the Staff Manual respectively. Title Pages will be prepared in manuscript.

Place	Date	Hour	Summary of Events and Information	Remarks and references to Appendices
FRICES	APRIL 1st		Damage done from No 8 feet 2.	
"	2		Franks cast broken, Swing cam in Clutch handle and frame twisted. Repairs smaller about £50.	Offr
"	3		Lost damage others estimate at about £50.	Offr
"	4		Returned on Carpks since there. Allowed ½ leave 3 every Thursday. FP to a few men not to be awarded by CSM.	DJAG 9HQ.
"	5		Medical Inspection every Thursday fortnight at 2 p.m. Men who so want to take in place of volunteer.	Offr.
F	31			

WAR DIARY
or
INTELLIGENCE SUMMARY

(Erase heading not required.)

Army Form C. 2118

Place	Date	Hour	Summary of Events and Information	Remarks and references to Appendices
FRUGES	6		When measuring pumps hands on 200P Daiso Cars are fixed to taken Breeches the front screw first	Sgt Cpl 144 SRo m97
			Glasses not for P.H. helmets.	
			Heat ration 60% Hypo (1lb.) 25% P.H. (3/to) 15% H.H. (3 any and 1/7) P+B (4 — 7/8 3 ration parties.	C/m
	7		Leave in future 6 days clear in England 2 days for travelling Gate houses the provided with rest rape. Wire gauges to Manes from 8th Oct.	S.Ro. 1087 C/m
	8		Leave ratio for the month 13th; 20th; 27th (3)	C/m

WAR DIARY
INTELLIGENCE SUMMARY

Army Form C. 2118

Place	Date	Hour	Summary of Events and Information	Remarks and references to Appendices
FRUGES	10		Extracts from General Memoranda by D.f.T. received. Note oil reservoir on lorries leaking - sparking plugs. Unnecessary wearing of Overalls for Spare Parts &c clothing	GM
"	11		A.F. W 3338 to be rendered in duplicate. One car struck off establishment.	GM
"	12		S/Sgt Hicks returned from leave. Two reinforcements sent out as escort.	GM 141
"	13		N.C.O. improvements for Killer Accident Genston. All men detailed were on leave before on 18th.	
"	14		Cpl ___ returned to Ordnance	GM

WAR DIARY
or
INTELLIGENCE SUMMARY

(Erase heading not required.)

Army Form C. 2118

Place	Date	Hour	Summary of Events and Information	Remarks and references to Appendices
FRUGES	15th		Correspondence with Chargers Potations	020 1090
			Auburn & Triumph Catalogues received	Cpl.
"	16		Special Packing Cases in future will be marked "Return to Base"	AAC 1224
			New Vehicle Deposits personnel tests received	
"	17		Motor Cycles not to be sent by rail re with any petrol or oil in the Tanks	8047 10893
"	18		Leaf Samples returned from leave	Cpl.
			Leave not started to certain places in Lancashire & Durham	Cpl.

Army Form C. 2118

WAR DIARY
or
INTELLIGENCE SUMMARY
(Erase heading not required.)

Place	Date	Hour	Summary of Events and Information	Remarks and references to Appendices
FRUGES	20		Taupe roads the report on MT recepts rooms	Diary T.292.
"	21st		Stories of SO Woodruff & Notion Officers School contain full detail. Thou the maline is scheduled.	
			6 Gunners Report to OC ASC at 10AM Monday at HEZECQUES WOOD.	
"	22		Rations to be drawn for consumption on 25th. Leave broken on 26th. Bow 4.20 pm.	
"	24		Villages of BRIMEAUX & BEAUMERIE placed out of bounds owing to Scarlet fever. In a Court martial for Disobedience of Repeated Standing Orders. Drivers unable give Show Stable Orders were published.	

WAR DIARY
or
INTELLIGENCE SUMMARY
(Erase heading not required.)

Army Form C. 2118

Place	Date	Hour	Summary of Events and Information	Remarks and references to Appendices
FRUGES	25th		Inspected tyres. One requiring renewal. Remainder in good condition	GPC
"	26th		Sanctioned works evacuated unless quite beyond repair by units. Reserve of demolition explosives to be kept at Railhead	G.R.O. 2009
"	27		Only one copy of A.F. 3401 is to be sent to D.B.R.O. with each Billeting Requisite. A second copy should be left with the mine. 4 officers in M.T.	D.A.T. AC 1319
"	28		No applications for transfer acceptable in future. A Broad Arrow to be placed on the registration plate of each motor bicycle	

Army Form C. 2118

WAR DIARY
or
INTELLIGENCE SUMMARY
(Erase heading not required.)

Instructions regarding War Diaries and Intelligence Summaries are contained in F. S. Regs., Part II. and the Staff Manual respectively. Title Pages will be prepared in manuscript.

Place	Date	Hour	Summary of Events and Information	Remarks and references to Appendices
FRUGES	29		Capt. W.C. Sampler ordered to report to D of S + T War office for duty with new Armies. 2nd/(temp Lt.) E. McMahon to join from 2 G.H.Q Res Park.	A.G.H.Q. G/M.
"	30		Re-promotion of N.C.O's. Letter A.G., G.r. No. 14/1916.	A.G. H.Q. Fr.w

J. Nudatten ff Asst
for D.C.
No 3 Cav Am Park.

WAR DIARY
or
INTELLIGENCE SUMMARY
(Erase heading not required.)

Army Form C. 2118

Summary of Ammunition Received and Issued.

Date	Hour	Rec'd from.	Nature	No. of Rounds	Date	Issued to.	Nature	No. of Rounds
2/4/16		Seraycele	Mills Grenade	1008	9/4/16	1st Royal Dragoons	Mills Grenade	120
6/4/16		M.Cooks Am. Park.	"	900	"	2nd Dragoon Gds.	"	108
6/4/16		do	Large Lights	300	"	Somerset Yeo	"	108
13/4/16		D.O. Boulogne	Large Lights	1000	"	Ryl. Horse Gds	"	108
"		"	Rifle Grenade	100	"	10th Roy. Hussars	"	120
29/4/16		H'cooks Amm. Park.	Mills Grenade (Army)	1000	"	Essex Yeo	"	108
					"	1st Life Gds	"	108
					"	2nd Life Gds	"	120
					"	Leicester Yeo	"	108
					15/4/16	Div. School	Large Lights	300
					24/4/16	1st Cav. Bde.	Mills Grenade	300

WAR DIARY or INTELLIGENCE SUMMARY

Army Form C. 2118

Place	Date	Hour	Summary of Events and Information						Remarks and references to Appendices
			Receipts			**Issues**			
			From	Nature	No/yds	To	Nature	No/yds	
	4/4/16		1st Cav Bde	Mills Grenade	300	1st Cav Bde	Mills Grenade	300	
			"	"	"	10th Royal Hussars	"	100	
			"	"	"	Royal Horse Gds.	"	100	
			"	"	"	Essex Yeo	"	100	
		13/4/16	"	"	"	1st Royal Dragoons	Gas helmet Phelm	360	
			"	"	"	"	" 1½"	24	
			"	"	"	3rd Dragoon Gds	" 1"	360	
			"	"	"	"	" 1½"	24	
			"	"	"	Somerset Yeo	" 1"	360	
			"	"	"	"	" 1½"	24	
			"	"	"	1st Life Gds.	" 1"	360	
			"	"	"	"	" 1½"	24	
			"	"	"	2nd Life Gds.	" 1"	360	

WAR DIARY
or
INTELLIGENCE SUMMARY
(Erase heading not required.)

Army Form C. 2118

Instructions regarding War Diaries and Intelligence Summaries are contained in F.S. Regs., Part II. and the Staff Manual respectively. Title Pages will be prepared in manuscript.

Place	Date	Hour	Summary of Events and Information					Remarks and references to Appendices
			Issued	Nature	No/yds	Date	To	Issued
	3/4/16		To 2nd Life Guards	Cartridge Illum 18"	24	4/4/16	D.S. School	Cartridge Illum 18" 192
			" Royal Horse Gds.	"	360	"	"	Safety fuze 32 yds
			"	"	1½	7/4/16	6th M.C. Sqd.	Cartridge Very Pistol 108
			10th Royal Hussars	"	360	"	7th M.C. Sqd.	" 108
			"	"	1½	"	8th M.C. Sqd.	" 108
			Essex Yeo	"	360			
			"	"	1½			
			Leicester Yeo	"	360			
			"	"	1½			
	16/4/16		D.S. School	Cartridge Illum	1½			
			"	Rifle Grenades No 3	100			
			"	Mobel Sturm tinglers	600			

3C

Confidential

War Diary

of

3rd Cavalry Ammunition Park

From 1st May 1916 to 31st May 1916

(Volume 16)

WAR DIARY
or
INTELLIGENCE SUMMARY

(Erase heading not required.)

May

Army Form C. 2118

Place	Date	Hour	Summary of Events and Information	Remarks and references to Appendices
Fruges	1st	"	2nd Lt (Temp Lt) J N Watters reported for duty.	AQMG Trds
"	2nd	"		
"	3rd	"	Re-Wd leave can be granted to Ireland.	Re Wd TA2L. Trds.
"	4th	"	Capt Mark. proceeded on leave	
"	5th	"	Leave stopped to Plumhealh owing to outbreak of Measles	Re Wd TA3L. Trds.

Army Form C. 2118

WAR DIARY
or
INTELLIGENCE SUMMARY
(Erase heading not required.)

Instructions regarding War Diaries and Intelligence Summaries are contained in F.S. Regs., Part II. and the Staff Manual respectively. Title Pages will be prepared in manuscript.

Place	Date	Hour	Summary of Events and Information	Remarks and references to Appendices
Juyes	6th		Reached ARCQUES in Jubiter	
"	7th		Two reinforcement Tom from No 1 Base M.T. Depot consisting of 1 fitter & 1 Driver.	This
"	8th		Motor Driver returned with a log book but an additional column required of Officer using car. Signature of officer using war/ca in the mileage reign return with end of the Journey.	
"	9th			
"	10th		13 hour tobe drawn up	
"	11th			

Army Form C. 2118

WAR DIARY
or
INTELLIGENCE SUMMARY
(Erase heading not required.)

Place	Date	Hour	Summary of Events and Information	Remarks and references to Appendices
Fauges	12th		2/Lieut. R.H. Stevens goes on leave.	Offr
"	13th		Capt. Grant returned from leave.	
			Musketry training between drafts on the range.	
"	15		Inspected guns. In good order with one or two exceptions for causes of corrosion.	Gun
"	16		Pivot pins are not to be used for any purpose whatever	
			New books of Contents, Stores & Railway Warrants available	
			Ry establishment 25% of men driven out. Reformed one reserve 2 drivers per lorry.	Gen
	17		Lt McWatters proceeded on leave. Return on 26th	Offr
	18		Indent sent in for motor cycle to replace one returned etc.	
			No 19 Grenades became due. The nightly firing is to not fall out. The guns & the firing stores is of course 1st action shot stands at 100 ft throwing good.	Stop MG

1875 Wt. W593/826 1,000,000 4/15 J.B.C. & A. A.D.S.S./Forms/C. 2118.

Instructions regarding War Diaries and Intelligence Summaries are contained in F.S. Regs., Part II. and the Staff Manual respectively. Title Pages will be prepared in manuscript.

Army Form C. 2118

WAR DIARY
or
INTELLIGENCE SUMMARY
(Erase heading not required.)

Place	Date	Hour	Summary of Events and Information	Remarks and references to Appendices
FRUGES	19th		Received list of m/c cycles. Acknowledged 2nd Aust.; shot 5 rounds at post; shooting good.	Offr.
"	20		G. Stevens returned from leave. 1st Kirke 5 rolls April 30 G 2 Lt Stevens to do April 30 (a)	Offr.
"	21		Inspected weekly mileage. Average miles per gallon increased slightly.	Offr.
"	22		No on station shot 5 rounds.	

WAR DIARY
or
INTELLIGENCE SUMMARY

Army Form C. 2118.

Place	Date	Hour	Summary of Events and Information	Remarks and references to Appendices
ROUEN	23rd		1/4 Bn to proceed on leave/ spend in England. Value light Oloroso in Vandalls Lane Shawl hollow dar. 010 " " " .006. intr	DT CM 152 Офи
"	24	Bath 1.30 — 3 P.M.	Commencement for Oaths. Lt Col Mellor D.S.A.C OTR. Disobedience for men they not be loved to GO.	1589.
"	25		Regulations re private telegrams. repeat 1. Senders surname to Government. 2. Bell's Name Rank Inits. for reference. 3. Telegraphic addresses for British + General Solomon only. 4. Telegrams should be either typewritten or/ponciled in block letters.	Офи

1875 Wt. W593/826 1,000,000 4/15 J.B.C. & A. A.D.S.S./Forms/C. 2118.

WAR DIARY
or
INTELLIGENCE SUMMARY
(Erase heading not required.)

Army Form C. 2118

Place	Date	Hour	Summary of Events and Information	Remarks and references to Appendices
FRUGES	26		Lt. the Walters returned from leave.	Chart 9/20 2047.
	27		All Guard of leave to June 4.	
	28		Notes before may not to work on Cars. When a driver officer visits a Repair dept and orders claim the officer of the Repair succeed will accompany him.	Chart
	29		There is no such rank as Staff Sergeant in the M.T. as said in W.E. Sole. Stuff of cars having repairs are drawn occurs in front depot	ADT W.O. 10% 9S 9635.
	30		A/Lee returned to O.C. 3rd ARC Repair Shop closed to accompanied by the necessary road vouchers.	AuL 1385.

Army Form C. 2118

WAR DIARY
or
INTELLIGENCE SUMMARY
(Erase heading not required.)

Instructions regarding War Diaries and Intelligence Summaries are contained in F. S. Regs., Part II. and the Staff Manual respectively. Title Pages will be prepared in manuscript.

Place	Date	Hour	Summary of Events and Information	Remarks and references to Appendices
FRUGES	31.		Enfilorists should be relined. O'Ammunition Peabody.	C Martin Capt Quant 2nd in Com O.C.

1875 Wt. W 593/826 1,000,000 4/15 J.B.C. & A. A.D.S.S./Forms/C. 2118.

WAR DIARY
or
INTELLIGENCE SUMMARY of Ammunition Rec'd & Issued

Army Form C. 2118

(Erase heading not required.)

Place	Date	Hour	No Rounds	From Whom Received	Nature	Summary of Events and Information Date	No Rounds	To whom issued	Remarks and references to Appendices
Rouen	1/5/16		652	CO Boulogne	Pistol Webley	1/5/16	652	2 Cav Supply Column	Pistol Webley
"	"		1,006	"	Mills Grenades	2/5/16	3,000	Divisional School	303 324
"	"		100	"	Rifle .303	"	1,00	"	Rifle Grenades R.G.
"	"		1,000	"	Hotchkiss Rifle	"	3,00	"	Hotchkiss Rifle
"	9/5/16		511	3rd Dragoon Guards	Ball Grenades	5/5/16	150	10th Hussars	Cartridges R.Grenade
"	11/5/16		64	CO Boulogne	Phosphorus Grenades	7/5/16	9,000	"	B.Act 303
"	"		11.04	"	Pistol Rocket	"	500	"	Cartridges R.Grenade
"	13/5/16		1115	Div Training School	Ball Grenades	15/5/16	500 1120	O.C. Ammo Train	Detonators Mills F.
"	"		419	"	Mills Grenade	"	9	"	Grenades Rifle Pipe
"	"		111.	"	Rifle 303	"	38	"	Detonators "
"	"		10	"	" Pistol	"	40	"	" 303 R.44 G.
"	15/5/16		144	OC Amm Train	Grenades BM Gr	22/5/16	1,008	6th 4th and 5t Cav Bde	Grenades Rifle .05
"	24/5/16		7000	2nd Rifle Grenades	Cart "B" Rifle	26/5/16	20.	6 to Cav Bde	Guncotton Primers
"	24/5/16		20,000	Canadian Amm Park	S.A.A "B" Rifle	"	3 Yrms	"	Safety Fuze
						26/5/16	2.H.	"	Detonators 303

WAR DIARY
or
INTELLIGENCE SUMMARY
(Erase heading not required.)

Army Form C. 2118

Summary of Ammunition Received and Issued

Place	Date	Hour	Receipts			Issues			Remarks and references to Appendices
			Nature	No. of Rounds	Rec'd from	Nature	Date	No. of Rounds	Issued To	
Hugs.							24/5/16	48	9th Cav. Bde.	Nature
"				—			"	100 fd.	"	Web of wd-
							29/5/16	10,000	Essex Yeo.	24ft fuze
							29/5/16	1,360	North Somerset Yeo.	303 S.A.A.
							"	1,104	Royal Horse Guards	Pistol Webley
										Rich Webley

CONFIDENTIAL.

WAR DIARY

of

3rd Cavalry Ammunition Park.

From 1st June. 1916.   To 30th. June. 1916.

(Volume 17.)

Army Form C. 2118

WAR DIARY
or
INTELLIGENCE SUMMARY
(Erase heading not required.)

June.

Place	Date	Hour	Summary of Events and Information	Remarks and references to Appendices
FRUGES	1		Started mowing crop from Ryegrass & Rib about 1080 bundles a day. Each lorry taking on aver. of 50 bundles.	Offr.
	2		Sgt. White returned from leave. Men to pass for Hay horses 6.14. Tars 20.17. Syds 40.35.	Offr.
	3.		No Italian crop arms for Sudeans to andend for	A.A. 1370 O.M.ry 7364 O.C. A/C Offr. "Case
	4.		Leave reverts reversed to 2 per week.	
	5.		No leave exceed 7 days from time of leaving unit.	Offr. CM 156.
			Attention drawn to GRO 981 re shortage of whelo. had in trapes AFW 3346 "Effect of efficiency Report" the intended for	

WAR DIARY
or
INTELLIGENCE SUMMARY
(Erase heading not required.)

Army Form C. 2118

Place	Date	Hour	Summary of Events and Information	Remarks and references to Appendices
FRUGES	8	—	Divisional Baths closed.	RRJ 16/11
"	9		2 men to work relatable & ROQC acting and the word. Sharpman his arrival claimed to have not to exceed 3 Francs the.	JM.
"	10		Leave 7 days from [ ] of Embarkation between stopped Embarkation	EJ.
"	11		have to be taken that return half of passes are not lost.	JM.
"			9 Lorries moved to BERCK. MERLIMONT & CUCK to Transp. mechine of S.O. Bus to permanent lines	
			Mileage for the week Lorries 1198 Private 1918 galo. mi.p.g. = 6.27	
			Cars 414 " 20 " = 20.70	
			Cycles 308 " 7 " = 44.00	
"	12		MT Drivers are not to be left in charge or have evidence of any without the authority of the Corps Commander. A letter is his a notice to force fortesting any man start here (1) Roster (2) Roster.	JM.

WAR DIARY
or
INTELLIGENCE SUMMARY

(Erase heading not required.)

Army Form C. 2118

Place	Date	Hour	Summary of Events and Information	Remarks and references to Appendices
FRUGES	13		Officer in a motor accident may be held responsible if the accident is due to his order or negligence	A.C. 1422 A.G.3 5253 CJM
"	14		Bayleff cannot enmesh at stations. Clocks not moved from 11 to 12 midnight.	CJM
"	15		One man not let leave for a year owing to #7. Arms + Equipment of men reporting sick about accompany them to the DRS. On evacuation from DRS to a General or Stationary Hospital the arms + equipment will be handed in to Ordnance Stores.	CJM
"	16		W.O.s N.C.O.s + men are entitled to ration allces when on leave. A.R. 39(c)	3R.O. 286. CJM

Army Form C. 2118

WAR DIARY
or
INTELLIGENCE SUMMARY
(Erase heading not required.)

Instructions regarding War Diaries and Intelligence Summaries are contained in F.S. Regs., Part II. and the Staff Manual respectively. Title Pages will be prepared in manuscript.

Place	Date	Hour	Summary of Events and Information	Remarks and references to Appendices
RUGLES	17		Petrol Economy to be enforced by overhauling sections if necessary.	E Army S6589
"	18		QM stages from X A5 joined as W.O. L/Cpl Jones over from 175 with L O1/CRA Section of Training Coy.	Offr
			Petrol consumption Mileage	
				Petrol	m.P.G.
			Lorries 1956	308	6.35
			Cars 242	12	20.16
			Cycles 749	18	41.61	
	19.		GROs 1295 & 1436 to be read out on parade once a month on CCs 1st & 10th. Precautions against Fire.	Offr

1875 Wt. W593/826 1,000,000 4/15 J.B.C. & A. A.D.S.S./Forms/C. 2118.

WAR DIARY
or
INTELLIGENCE SUMMARY

Army Form C. 2118

Place	Date	Hour	Summary of Events and Information	Remarks and references to Appendices
FROLEN	25		Moved Gun from line to DOMART & PONTHIEU arriving 6pm. Convoy left Frolen at 1pm. Horse lines near Loft. One type off.	CfE
DOMART	26		Stayed night 25-26 in billets. Moved out at 1.30pm to LANEUVILLE. Reports O.C. XV Corps ordt. attached us LANEUVILLE - DAOURS road for Bivouac. Park arrived at 6pm.	CfE
LANEUVILLE	27		Bivouac pitched. Water obtained by carrying about ½ mile along DAOURS road. Latter two to a spring about a mile along DAOURS road.	CfE
"	28		Park now under Reserve Army Q for moves. " " " IV Army ADOS for Ammunition.	
"	29		Rations in future to be drawn from the B Echelon Dump.	

Marshe Capt
OC ? CAP

WAR DIARY
or
INTELLIGENCE SUMMARY
(Erase heading not required.)

Army Form C. 2118

Instructions regarding War Diaries and Intelligence Summaries are contained in F. S. Regs., Part II. and the Staff Manual respectively. Title Pages will be prepared in manuscript.

Place	Date	Hour	Summary of Events and Information	Remarks and references to Appendices
O L Bombay	29/6/16		Ammn: Receipts. 3 pr. A.R. 480 rds 3pr A.R. Ammn: Issues June. Ammunition Yeo 16,000 1.a.a. 303 10.6.16 — do — 8.2 5 — do — 10th R. Sussex 6,000 1.a.a. 303 19.6.16 R. Wedby — do — 6th M.G. Squd 6,000 1.a.a. 303 20.6.16 — do — 1104. R.Set. — do — 3rd B. Sqdn. 14,000 1.a.a. 303 21.6.16 — do — — do — 552 P. Web. — do — Pailhead Brymin 24,000 1.a.a. 303 — do — 4th Bde R.H.A. 6,000 1.a.a. 303 22.6.16 3rd L. Lancashire R. 1,000 1.a.a. 303 — do — 9th A.Bns B.S.F. 26 F. 3pr. a.R. 29.6.16	

Vol 18

Confidential

War Diary

—of—

3rd Cavalry Ammunition Park.

From 1st July 1916. To 31st July 1916.

(Volume 16.)

WAR DIARY
or
INTELLIGENCE SUMMARY
(Erase heading not required.)

Army Form C. 2118

Place	Date	Hour	Summary of Events and Information	Remarks and references to Appendices
HALLENCOURT	July 4		Moved from LONGUEVILLE at 4.30 AM & arrived here at 8.45 via AMIENS - PICQUIGNY HIRAINES.	Offr.
	5		Details arrived. Orderly room in tent.	
			Lorries reported. Latrines re-erected. Pipe in/where the collected & Sanitary Station.	Offr.
	7		Pack Mules. The men on all duties where arms are carried	Offr.
	8		Moved from HALLENCOURT to LONGUEVILLE via AMIENS & DREUX. Orders 17th arrived 6.15 p.m.	
	11		Signals the strength of movements 9 a.m. & 12 & after each call returned about except from 12-2 & 6-8 p.m.	Offr.
	13		Train for forward to Q. 10 u.70 until four reinforcements arrived	Offr.

Army Form C. 2118

WAR DIARY
or
INTELLIGENCE SUMMARY
(Erase heading not required.)

Instructions regarding War Diaries and Intelligence Summaries are contained in F.S. Regs., Part II. and the Staff Manual respectively. Title Pages will be prepared in manuscript.

Place	Date	Hour	Summary of Events and Information	Remarks and references to Appendices
LANDRVILLE	14		Attached to XIV Corps Park for duty. Reported to Col. Harvey & Commdt. Cyclist trainband to Zuytpeete Park for Ammunition.	Offr.
"	15		Recruits showed not to Ammnt Depot for small parts which can be worn in to shop.	Doty. 7856/10.
"	22		Lamps to be cleaned up daily whenever there being up behind in the vicinity of moves.	Arl 1297. Offr
"	23		Ammunition returned in lorries. Salvage parties detailed for shifting dumps in case of a move.	Offr
"	29		All tents to be camouflaged and tarpaulins exception. Sapper works Division will be made to III Corps for administration	2122 ERO. 2123
"	30		From the 28th the 3rd Cavalry Division will be under the III Corps for administration	Offrs

Army Form C. 2118

WAR DIARY
or
INTELLIGENCE SUMMARY

(Erase heading not required.)

Ammunition — July 1916.

Instructions regarding War Diaries and Intelligence Summaries are contained in F. S. Regs., Part II. and the Staff Manual respectively. Title Pages will be prepared in manuscript.

Place	Date	Hour	Summary of Events and Information				Remarks and references to Appendices
			Receipts	Date	Issues		
from :-							
O.C. Coventry	10-7-16		60,000 S.a.a. 303	10-7-16	42,000 S.a.a. 303	O.C. 6th Bde.	
O.C. Coventry	17-7-16		60,000 S.a.a. 303	15-7-16	21,000 S.a.a. 303	O.C. 8th Bde.	
O.C. Coventry	24-7-16		54,000 S.a.a. 303	16-7-16	9,000 S.a.a. 303	O.C. Lincoln Yeo.	
O.C. Coventry	25-7-16		6,000 S.a.a. 303	16-7-16	36,000 S.a.a. 303	O.C. 7th Bde.	
O.C. Coventry	29-7-16		32,000 S.a.a. 303	24-7-16	26,000 S.a.a. 303	O.C. 6th M. Gun Squadron	
O.C. Coventry	29-7-16		1,666,000 S.a.a. 303	28-7-16	60,000 S.a.a. 303	O.C. 8th Bde.	
				29-7-16	6,000 S.a.a. 303	O.C. N. Som. Yeo.	

Vol 19

Confidential

War Diary

of

3rd Cavalry Ammunition Park.

From 1st August 1916. To. 31st August 1916.

(Volume 19)

WAR DIARY
or
INTELLIGENCE SUMMARY

(Erase heading not required.)

Army Form C. 2118

Place	Date	Hour	Summary of Events and Information	Remarks and references to Appendices
LANEUVILLE	August 1	3 p.m.	Left here for ARGENVILLERS. Motor supply difficult. Sent to CAOURS about 6 kilometre before empty.	CJW
ARGENVILLERS	2.		Attached to 9th Corps Reserve Army for administration. Returning out staff of Gr. 9th Corps for Army Park. DDST of Reserve Army.	CJW
	3.		Reported to OC 9th Corps Annex: Paris at 4 PM and ger at DOMART in PONTHIEU. Rear details removed unreported [illegible] ordered owing to overstating on journey from LANEUVILLE. Refreshments continued in evening. Received orders at 2 AM to proceed to FRUGES at 3 PM and annex FRUGES at 6.30 PM.	CJW
FRUGES	4.		Left ARGENVILLERS at 3 PM and annex FRUGES at 6.30 PM.	CJW

WAR DIARY
or
INTELLIGENCE SUMMARY

(Erase heading not required.)

Army Form C. 2118

Instructions regarding War Diaries and Intelligence Summaries are contained in F. S. Regs., Part II. and the Staff Manual respectively. Title Pages will be prepared in manuscript.

Place	Date	Hour	Summary of Events and Information	Remarks and references to Appendices
FRANCE	6		NCOs reported as WOs3 appointed to Rosters Establishments cannot be recognised.	Offr.
"	7	6	Under instructions from H.Q. Fifth Reserve Army this Park has become Divisional Troops & is under the administration of	1/X postal R. 69.
			O.C. Arc. Distributed to all officers copy of Army Order 7/5: leakage of information. On leaving their offices	Offr.
"	8		Discipline in Billets. Broken. Officers will go round with the party closing the Barrack room is correct.	GRO 79
				Offr.
"	9		Applications for rectification of Service as filled in to be submitted to D-A-I Reserve Army. Bonus pay to contract drivers & others if entitled.	Offr.
"	10		Vehicles issued to KofC should be indicated & Lent to 5th Army. (Pilot) Boy Arc.	2953 461.
			Fires. When a fire occurs the APM should be informed as soon as possible of the fact of the Fire as may other evidence	GRO 2136.

Army Form C. 2118

WAR DIARY
or
INTELLIGENCE SUMMARY
(Erase heading not required.)

Instructions regarding War Diaries and Intelligence Summaries are contained in F. S. Regs., Part II. and the Staff Manual respectively. Title Pages will be prepared in manuscript.

Place	Date	Hour	Summary of Events and Information	Remarks and references to Appendices
FRUGES	14		Informed by DDFW Reserve Army that we are now under administration of GHQ.	Clln.
"	16		Returns to be rendered as on former occasions.	Clln.
"	18		Received circular on sanitation. Regret inspections be made. Lt W J Smith transferred to 55 Division "D" Battery 157 Bde. On remaining a while other han on drivers with only to send.	Clln. Clln. BRO 2149.
"	19		One returned with the attachment. No correspondence is to be despatched by troops arriving at work except through the Army P.O. Consignments of unused spare parts ought to Cal of Albinas to be returned GNOZ BMT Dept CALAIS or " " ROUEN.	Clln. Clln. CM 104
"	21		Ammunition U.S. 15" munitions for Hotchkiss guns to be returned. Sounds tank boxes are making some use of what is bracketed. (Letter M)	Clln.

Army Form C. 2118

WAR DIARY
or
INTELLIGENCE SUMMARY
(Erase heading not required.)

Instructions regarding War Diaries and Intelligence Summaries are contained in F.S. Regs, Part II. and the Staff Manual respectively. Title Pages will be prepared in manuscript.

Place	Date	Hour	Summary of Events and Information	Remarks and references to Appendices
FRUGES	21		Give in [?] re orders the brought to II notice of all reinforcements joining.	9Po 9SA 91.
"	22		Lorries into workshop village. These were brushed into with damaged plugs.	CM 97A
	23		W.O. woo's over north trench issued to LOC. Sent 1 ASC officer the return of QMG etc on the lorry of each unit.	2158 DRO QMG NotsC SJ06
	24		Patrol cars the thined to railhead. R.A.J. U.S. 15" Shis used for parades purposes.	Офи 2.52. Офо.
	28		Cars the disposal of base daily.	Офи.

1875 Wt. W593/826 1,000,000 4/15 J.B.C. & A. A.D.S.S./Forms/C. 2118.

Army Form C. 2118

WAR DIARY
or
INTELLIGENCE SUMMARY

(Erase heading not required.)

Instructions regarding War Diaries and Intelligence Summaries are contained in F.S. Regs., Part II. and the Staff Manual respectively. Title Pages will be prepared in manuscript.

Place	Date	Hour	Summary of Events and Information	Remarks and references to Appendices
FRUGES	29		Billets & Gillhem unchanged.	19/F
	30		ditto.	19/P
	31		ditto.	19/P.

J.Nash Capt.
for O.C. 3.e.a.P.

Army Form C. 2118

WAR DIARY
or
INTELLIGENCE SUMMARY
(Erase heading not required.)

Ammunition Issues — June 1916

Place	Date	Hour	Summary of Events and Information	Remarks and references to Appendices
Lake	12-6-16	O.E.	Receipts — Argus 2208 Pistol Webley	
	29-6-16	O.E.	Argus 2208 Pistol Webley	
	12-8-16	O.E.	Argus 25000 S.A.A. ".303"	
	29-8-16	O.O.	Boulogne 33000 — do —	
	10-8-16	O.O.	Boulogne 1000 Grenades Mills No.5	
			Issues	
			5572 Pistol Webley O.C. 4th Bde R.H.A.	7-6-16
			2256 — do — O.C. 3rd D. Guards	11-6-16
			825 — do — O.C. 4th Bde A.C. R.H.A.	16-6-16
			276 — do — A.P.M. 3rd Cav Div.	23-6-16
			625 — do — O.C. 4th Bde A.C. R.H.A.	24-6-16
			55.2 — do — O.C. N. Som Yeo	27-6-16
			276 — do — O.C. 3rd Cav Div Pk	31-5-16
			25000 S.A.A. ".303" O.C. 3rd D. Guards	11-6-16
			2000 — do — O.C. Royal Horse Guards	13-6-16
			2000 — do — 2nd Royals	13-6-16
			14000 — do — 2nd N. Som Yeo	21-6-16
			2000 — do — 2nd — do —	23-6-16
			7000 — do — 2nd Supply Column	25-6-16
			2000 — do — 2nd 3rd Cdn Army Pack	25-6-16
			1000 — do — 2nd 6th Coy S. Lgn.	27-6-16
			4000 — do — 2nd N. Som Yeo	27-6-16
			5000 — do — 2nd 3rd D. Guards	28-6-16
			1000 — do — 2nd No. 13 Mob Vet Sec	28-6-16
			2000 — do — 2nd Royals	28-6-16
			10000 — do — 2nd N. Som Yeo	29-6-16
			336 Grenades Mills O.C. 6th Cav Bde	11-6-16
			336 — do — O.C. 7th Cav Bde	11-6-16
			336 — do — O.C. 8th Cav Bde	

WAR DIARY
or
INTELLIGENCE SUMMARY
(Erase heading not required.)

Army Form C. 2118

Instructions regarding War Diaries and Intelligence Summaries are contained in F. S. Regs., Part II. and the Staff Manual respectively. Title Pages will be prepared in manuscript.

Place	Date	Hour	Summary of Events and Information	Remarks and references to Appendices
O.O Boulogne	10-6-16		Receipts 100 Grenadier Rifle no 3	
O.E Argyles	25-6-16		250 Romans Chandler	
			23.6.16 N Som gas -100 Grenadier Rifle no 3	
			28.8.16 Royals 100 — do	
			23.8.16 2.0 Bows & Gins 104 — do	
			24-8-16 2.0 "C" Bty Pla Burbridge Sham 1"	
			24-8-16 2.0 6th Bows Pda 50 Rahman Chandler	
			27-8-16 2.0 do 4th — do — 50 — do	
			29-8-16 2.0 do 6 do — do — do — 50	

Vol 20

Confidential
War Diary
of
3rd Cavalry Ammunition Park

From 1st September 1916 To 30th September 1916.

(Volume 20)

WAR DIARY
or
INTELLIGENCE SUMMARY

Army Form C. 2118

Place	Date	Hour	Summary of Events and Information	Remarks and references to Appendices
FPO 643	4		As many DRO's Cases no positive should be returned	DRO 299.
	7		Attention is drawn to the danger of drinking unfiltered or unboiled water. The Park being without a water cart all water must be boiled.	Offg DRO 286. O.Cr Car Cos O.Cr
	10		Empty Potato Sacks to be returned to railhead	
			* tank since obtained O.Cr	

WAR DIARY
or
INTELLIGENCE SUMMARY

(Erase heading not required.)

Army Form C. 2118

Instructions regarding War Diaries and Intelligence Summaries are contained in F.S. Regs., Part II. and the Staff Manual respectively. Title Pages will be prepared in manuscript.

Place	Date	Hour	Summary of Events and Information	Remarks and references to Appendices
GUESCHART	11th		Moved from FRUGES there: Billets.	
BELLOY SUR SOMME	12th		Moved from GUESCHART there. Billets	2nd Army IV Army
"	13th		Returned to E.T. McWalter Johnston	
BUSSYLES DAOURS – ALLONVILLE Road – 62 H25 a 79	14th		Moved from BELLOY SUR SOMME } Completed attack H.T. Coy with Coofa in Bivouac. 135D Rifle H.E. 1364 135D " Shrapnel 13/04 10 OD. Nosecaps Hotchkiss. 534,000 S.A.A.	Co. Corps Sig. G.R.O. 111.
"	15		Received Code letters for unloaded Ammunition. Bolts to be removed from rifles before cleaning takes place. Accidental injuries caused by detonators fuzes re. The retention of such articles is forbidden in future any NCO or man injuring himself through neglect to comply will be courtmartialled.	9/20 113.

Army Form C. 2118

WAR DIARY
or
INTELLIGENCE SUMMARY
(Erase heading not required.)

Instructions regarding War Diaries and Intelligence Summaries are contained in F.S. Regs., Part II. and the Staff Manual respectively. Title Pages will be prepared in manuscript.

Place	Date	Hour	Summary of Events and Information	Remarks and references to Appendices
62D A25 a 9.9	18		Return showing homes not being used to send in A.P.D. S.v.S/Ser. Corps on 13th of each month	D.o.1.7. a.v.o 8912/13.
			18th of each month	
"	19		Division of Army Pay Office. F.2.E.	ERO 1798.
			(a) H.T. supply, ration returns	
			(b) M T section	
			Separate Acquittance Rolls therent.	
			T.II Orders to be sent each brand	
			Transfers of NCOs & Men not the extra careful unless in the service, of Turnwine	180 S.
"	20		Hair & lachrymator munitions may be stored with other munitions of the	Q.o.S. 1/1/13
			Category but will they belong.	
			Incendiary & smoke munitions to be stored apart from explosive munitions	

Army Form C. 2118

WAR DIARY
or
INTELLIGENCE SUMMARY
(Erase heading not required.)

Instructions regarding War Diaries and Intelligence Summaries are contained in F.S. Regs., Part II. and the Staff Manual respectively. Title Pages will be prepared in manuscript.

Place	Date	Hour	Summary of Events and Information	Remarks and references to Appendices
(2D H29a/9	21		Orders received that Division moves W of AMIENS. This Park to stay in present bivouac & move straight into new area on 23rd.	S720
			Gun stores returned from Corps H.T. Coy.	2205
			Ration point proceeding on leave to be examined for scabies prior to going has been established at FRECHENCOURT.	SRO 9/4 20/4
VILLERS L'HOPITAL	23		Moved here today via Berguneper. Dept H.25a79 at 17H arrived here at 5PM. No casualties	Off.
HAUTEVILLE	24		Left VILLERS L'HOPITAL at 12PM arrived here at 2PM went into billets. Troops/brings. Lt. Col. W. Holded to facilitate transition of a break	Off.

1875 Wt. W593/826 1,000,000 4/15 J.B.C. & A. A.D.S.S./Forms/C. 2118.

Army Form C. 2118

WAR DIARY
or
INTELLIGENCE SUMMARY

(Erase heading not required.)

Instructions regarding War Diaries and Intelligence Summaries are contained in F. S. Regs., Part II. and the Staff Manual respectively. Title Pages will be prepared in manuscript.

Place	Date	Hour	Summary of Events and Information	Remarks and references to Appendices
HAUTEVILLE	25- 27		Billets remain the same.	Offr.
"	28		M.O. inspected camp. Inspected ablution trenches as common mess for company. Arrangements for these made by section Section officers.	Offr. Recce Offr. No 1 Area No H/157
	30		Stores for training purposes have to be consulted first. Picquet has to be returned complete with all pegs.	90/S 27 Offr.

Army Form C. 2118

WAR DIARY
or
INTELLIGENCE SUMMARY
(Erase heading not required.)

Instructions regarding War Diaries and Intelligence Summaries are contained in F. S. Regs., Part II. and the Staff Manual respectively. Title Pages will be prepared in manuscript.

Ammunition September 1916

Place	Date Hour	Summary of Events and Information	Remarks and references to Appendices
		Receipts	
O L Contay	15-9-16	Q F 18pr Shrapnel	1352
O L Contay	14-9-16	Q F 13pr H E	1348
O O Boulogne	4-9-16	S a a. .303 Ball	60.000
— do —	8-9-16	— do —	40.000
O D Beka	10-9-16	— do —	30.000
O L Contay	14-9-16	— " —	20.000
— do —	15-9-16	— " —	20.000
— do —	20-9-16	— " —	534.000
O O Boulogne	4-9-16	Pistol Webley	6
— do —	8-9-16	— do —	276
— do —	7-9-16	Grenades Mills no 5	1932
O C Beka	10-9-16	— do —	552
O L Contay	14-9-16	— do —	276
O D Boulogne	4-9-16	Grenade Rifle no 20	100
O C Beka	10-9-16	— do — no 3	260
O L Contay	19-9-16	Q F 3pr A P	64
a a + Q m F	17-9-16	Flares Verts	1000

		Issues	
O C	Amm + Transport 14-9-16	Q F 13pr	1352
O C	do 14-9-16	Q F 13pr H E	1348
O C	4th Pde A Col 3-9-16	S a a .303	60.000
O C	do 4-9-16	do	40.000
O C	do 6-9-16	N S Y 16	30.000
O C	80th Fd Amb Guards 8-9-16		20.000
O C	2nd Life Guards 6-9-16		21.000
O C	Amm + Transport 14-9-16		10
O C	4th Pde A Col 20-9-16		534.000
O C	3rd Cav Am Park 1-9-16	Pistol Webley	276
O C	4th Pde Am Col 3-9-16	— do —	1932
O C	9th L Arm Car Bty 6-9-16	— do —	552
O C	Q 6 Car Bde 14-9-16	— do —	276
O C	7th 3rd Car Div 17-9-16	— do —	552
O C	2nd Life Guards 8-9-16	— do —	276
O C	4th Pde Am Col 9-9-16	— do —	9960
O C	9th L Arm Car Bty 9-9-16	— do —	16 576
O C	6 Car Res 5-9-16	Grenade Mills	336
O C	9th Car Res 6-9-16	— do —	336
O C	9th Car Res 10-9-16	— do —	336
O C	3rd D Grenades 19-9-16	— do —	120
O C	Amm + Transport 14-9-16	— " — Rifle	180
O C	3rd D Grenades 14-9-16	— " —	260
	8-9-16	Q F 3pr A P	48

Quartermaster Cart
3rd Bde R of A
J.B.C.&A.

Vol 21

Confidential
War Diary
—of—

3rd Cavalry Ammunition Park.

From 1st October 1916.   To 31st October 1916.

(Volume 21.)

WAR DIARY
or
INTELLIGENCE SUMMARY
(Erase heading not required.)

Army Form C. 2118

Place	Date	Hour	Summary of Events and Information	Remarks and references to Appendices
HAUTEVILLE	Oct. 1		Billets reached the same.	Offr.
"	2		Lecture by A.D.M.S. 3rd Can. Div. on Trophic	Offr
"	3		Control	
"	4		Riders same.	
"	"		ADVD of REGNIERE-ECLUSE. Inoculated with T.A.B. in this unit 44 %. Charge ? Division 70 %. As many men as possible to be inoculated.	Offr.
"	5		Regiments completed with 1st Gen. Illuminaty; 6 hrs. to 1st regiment.	Offr.
"	6		Instructions received that no Acting ranks may be confirmed in any unit of the old Army	R/259/A b.o.t if one per

Army Form C. 2118

WAR DIARY
or
INTELLIGENCE SUMMARY
(Erase heading not required.)

Instructions regarding War Diaries and Intelligence Summaries are contained in F.S. Regs., Part II. and the Staff Manual respectively. Title Pages will be prepared in manuscript.

Place	Date	Hour	Summary of Events and Information	Remarks and references to Appendices
HAUTEVILLE	7		Billets remain the same	Offr
"	8		LAH may be spared from PACQUES.	
"	9		Intents for Gov't Store to be signed by Commanding Officer.	Offr GRO 2223
"	10		Visit of inspection by Lt Col Taneroff D.A.O. A&SAT Territorials. Record of conveniences states to be kept.	
"	11		Mechanical Inspection next Park. Spraying shops into town in two cases. Bevel Pinion rule in two cases. No but flap in own lorry. Clutch shafts 6.	Offr
"	12		Special leave granted for those who stayed in England on U.T.M.	
"	13		Guard to be supplied for the Civil Sunday.	
"	14		Corporal Moored with a single clerk. Employed as Post Officer required.	

1875 Wt. W593/826 1,000,000 4/15 J.B.C. & A. A.D.S.S./Forms/C. 2118.

WAR DIARY or INTELLIGENCE SUMMARY

Army Form C. 2118

Place	Date	Hour	Summary of Events and Information	Remarks and references to Appendices
HAUTEVILLE	16		Passed out, caused no CO's others riding motor cycle.	Offr.
"	17		Daimler car returned for the fitting of a new spring. Jars of glass bottles are required at the base for returns to England. They should be returned to H.Q. the supply column for Canofs.	SCO 3240. Offr.
"	18		Small pierced steel surface plate on chokes plug be removed. The hole should be replaced with plug washer in the original position. This matter is being taken up direct by ADVS for Corps.	Offr.
	20		Moved to WAILLY. OBN action following on 20".	SCO 1879
WAILLY	20		Any person found in possession of ammunition captured will be prosecuted for having it in his possession	

WAR DIARY
or
INTELLIGENCE SUMMARY
(Erase heading not required.)

Army Form C. 2118

Instructions regarding War Diaries and Intelligence Summaries are contained in F. S. Regs., Part II. and the Staff Manual respectively. Title Pages will be prepared in manuscript.

Place	Date	Hour	Summary of Events and Information	Remarks and references to Appendices
WALY.	24		13th Section SHAVERNAY proceed to 13th Car Coi: who hatho in charge. 8 Lorries required daily for refugees, including 1 lorry to St Louis.	Ch.
"	25		One lorry attached DREW at MONTREUIL Station	Ch.
"	26		Horses SAUPIGNEUL LES PETITES. Sgt MONTREUIL returned.	Ch.
"	27		Proposed Q. Cease temporals	Ch.
"	28		Beach training	
"	29		Received list of lorry horses showing no minimum weight of various details issued Station Officers.	Ch.
"	30		A/Cpl Kichwater the temporary Sgt from 1st Oct 16.	Ch.
"	31		Return of extraneous duty the car in weekly to start on Friday.	Ch.

1875 Wt. W593/826 1,000,000 4/15 J.B.C. & A. A.D.S.S./Forms/C. 2118.

Army Form C. 2118

WAR DIARY
or
INTELLIGENCE SUMMARY
(Erase heading not required.)

Place	Date	Hour	Summary of Events and Information	Remarks and references to Appendices
CAMP PICARDIE LES PETITES	31.		Mileage for the month & petrol consumption	
			Miles Petrol M.P.G.	
			Lorries 7388 1220 6.05	
			Cars 2668 147 18.14	
			Cycles 2235 55 40.45	
			3/7 Charles Gill	
			OC 3 CAP	

WAR DIARY or INTELLIGENCE SUMMARY

Army Form C. 2118

Ammunition October 1916 3rd C.A. Park

Place	Date	Hour	Summary of Events and Information	Remarks and references to Appendices
			Receipts	
10-10-16	O.E.	Argues	Q.F. 18pr. H.E.	5
10-10-16	O.E.	Argues	S.A.A. 303" Ball	14000
14-10-16	O.E.	Argues	" "	10000
22-10-16	O.D.	Boulogne	" "	62000
10-10-16	O.E.	Argues	Pistol Webley	2208
14-10-16	O.E.	Argues	Grenades Mills no. 5	12
22-10-16	O.D.	Boulogne	" "	36
11-10-16	O.D.	Boulogne	Cart. G. Illum. 1"	2500+
			Issues	
	3-X-16	D.C.	4th 13pr Bde Amn Col Q.F. 13pr H.E.	5
	5-X-16	D.C.	6th M.G. Sqnd SAA 303"	2000
	5-X-16	D.C.	Army ,, ,,	7000
	6-X-16	D.C.	Army ,, ,,	5000
	13-X-16	D.C.	N. Som ,, ,,	10000
	19-X-16	D.C.	Yeo. M.G. Sqnd ,, ,,	12000
	19-X-16	D.C.	2nd Life Guards ,,	11000
	19-X-16	D.C.	4th Bde Amn Col ,,	10000
	19-X-16	D.C.	N. Som ,, ,,	20000
	20-X-16	D.C.	6th M.G. Sqnd ,,	8000
	5-X-16	D.C.	1st Life Guards Pistol Webley	528
	19-X-16	D.C.	4th & 13th Bde Amn Col ,,	524
	22-X-16	D.C.	6th Cav Bde ,,	296
	14-X-16	D.C.	Essex Yeo Grenades Mills no. 5	826
	19-X-16	D.C.	2nd Life Guards ,,	12
	1-X-16	D.C.	4th M.G. Guards Cart G Illum 1 1/2"	36
	6-X-16	D.D.	Army yeo Cart "Illum 1" "Parachute"	24
	5-X-16	D.C.	10th Regt Grenades do	450
	5-X-16	D.C.	R.F. Grenades do	450
	5-X-16	D.C.	1st Life Grenades do	450
	5-X-16	D.C.	Essex Yeo do	450
	5-X-16	D.C.	2nd Life Grenades do	450
	5-X-16	D.C.	1st Royals Grenades do	450
	5-X-16	D.C.	N.S.Y.H.Q. do	1
	5-X-16	D.C.	3rd Bde Grenades do	450

Vol 22

Confidential
War Diary
of
3rd Cavalry Ammunition Park
From 1st November 1916 to 30th November 1916.

Volume 22.

WAR DIARY
or
INTELLIGENCE SUMMARY
(Erase heading not required.)

Army Form C. 2118

Place	Date	Hour	Summary of Events and Information	Remarks and references to Appendices
CAMPIGNEUL LES PETITES	November 1		Collected bombed from FRUGES 17-fold time.	Offrs
"	2		Capt. O.J. Mealin and Lieut. J.P.H. Stevens attended court of enquiry held at Wailly.	J.P. J.P.
"	3		C.Q.M.S. left for Rouen, to visit sick wards.	J.P. C.L.
"	4		Sims Lewis to Boulogne, Petit Trailu CRE. One to bar leafs.	J.P.
"	5		Sims Lewis to our café. 1 day to RE Montreuil.	J.P.
"	6		Railhead to Lillers unchanged	J.P.
"	7		One Lorry lorries REs: C.Q.M.S. returned from Rouen -	J.P.
"	8		Advanced section returned. 10.30 pm.	J.P.
"	9		Lt. J.H. Stevens attended F.G.C.M. at Wailly.	J.P.
"	10		Stations Railhead to Lillers unchanged.	J.P.
"	11		Tape/mark returned Portbon of absence.	Offrs.
"	12		Shackett cover to be renewed.	Ofr.
			NCOs & officers the best of the School for instruction Ammunition dump started. Thos. made of Stone.	

Army Form C. 2118

WAR DIARY
or
INTELLIGENCE SUMMARY
(Erase heading not required.)

Instructions regarding War Diaries and Intelligence Summaries are contained in F. S. Regs., Part II. and the Staff Manual respectively. Title Pages will be prepared in manuscript.

Place	Date	Hour	Summary of Events and Information	Remarks and references to Appendices
CAMPICNUR LE 17871750	15		Have offered. One man posted. Road discipline & traffic control. Convoy to be divided into sections of 6 + 25 & distance to be kept. Vehicle Regist. checked by Brens branch.	APO. PM9. 1943. Offr.
	16		3 16zin small 21 NAAFI had arrived.	Offr
	17		Instructions received for 600 Nissen Huts to OC 491 Coy. Lt-Col. Prescot British Line.	
	18		No MT vehicles are to be executed without authority of DADOS.	Offr.
	20		Lt Prescott from 25 ACP returned home. Capt. Kirk proceeded to 491 Coy Heavy Anti-Tank Armr Park & Tanks.	

1875 Wt. W593/826 1,000,000 4/15 J.B.C. & A. A.D.S.S./Forms/C. 2118.

WAR DIARY or INTELLIGENCE SUMMARY

Army Form C. 2118

Place	Date	Hour	Summary of Events and Information	Remarks and references to Appendices
HAMINCOURT LES PETITES	22		NISSEN HUT SERVICE. Captain Walter proceed on leave.	Offr
	23		Orders received for to Heavy Batteries OC 654 Bay Arc XIV Corps Heavy Artillery at MEAULTE. 2Lt Harris from XI SC to report here.	Offr
			Lt Pleven will stoner & crews of two RE lorries.	Offr
	26		Drew two lorries from 2nd Aux Spares.	
	28		4 Drivers left Park to report SDC 6548ay Arc (15 Siege Bty) a/c/ Hd qr XIV Army Corps Heavy Artillery.	ADC 1757. DADS 180. A.G. A.18532
			2L & 1 Driver from 11 Div SC reported.	
			5y. wo. refixed as at POL	
			Authorised scale of Equipment for motor vehicles.	
			Recruits required for MGC Heavy Section	

WAR DIARY
or
INTELLIGENCE SUMMARY

(Erase heading not required.)

Army Form C. 2118

Instructions regarding War Diaries and Intelligence Summaries are contained in F.S. Regs., Part II. and the Staff Manual respectively. Title Pages will be prepared in manuscript.

Place	Date	Hour	Summary of Events and Information	Remarks and references to Appendices
CHAPIGNEULES LESPITES	30		Summary of Petrol consumption & miles per gallon for November.	
			MILES Gals M.P.G.	
			5855 945 6.00 lorries	
			2964 169 17.55 cars	
			2058 52 39.57 cycles	
				E.J. Marlin Cole O.C. 3 C.M.B.

Army Form C. 2118

WAR DIARY
or
INTELLIGENCE SUMMARY

(Erase heading not required.)

Instructions regarding War Diaries and Intelligence Summaries are contained in F. S. Regs., Part II. and the Staff Manual respectively. Title Pages will be prepared in manuscript.

Place	Date	Hour	Summary of Events and Information	Remarks and references to Appendices
			Ammunition November 1916	
			Issues	
			Receipts	
			25-11-16 B.G 6th M.G Sqdn S.A.A 303	360,000
			5-11-16 C.M.G 8th M.G Sqdn Bristol Sopp'y	828
			8-11-16 D.G 7th G'pr Box — " —	296
			25-11-16 B.G 8th G.M G' ne — " —	1360
			25-11-16 B.G 7th G.M G' ne Cart Illum'n	30

Vol 23.

Confidential
War Diary
of
3rd Cavalry Ammunition Park.
From 1st December 1916 to 31st December 1916.

(Volume 23)

WAR DIARY
or
INTELLIGENCE SUMMARY

(Erase heading not required.)

Army Form C. 2118

Place	Date	Hour	Summary of Events and Information	Remarks and references to Appendices
CAMP PIGNEULES LES PETITES	DECEMBER			
	2.		Sapper Watkin ADC returned from leave. L/Cpl Prescott proceeded on leave.	Ofr.
	4.		Orders regarding extinguishing of lights on the approach of hostile Aircraft. Sentry posted in Orderly Room. Patrol arranged.	Ofr. Ofr.
	5.		Private payment to troops by men in fortnight.	
	6.		Ablution benches issued to 2nd BMT Deptr. 151 " " Deniles " " Issue of 10,000 SAA, 303 Islands per week approved.	O.C. 9/605
	7.		26 men & 50 horses the billets in the village attached for rations.	Ofr.
	10.		Divisional sign the painted over all the lorries. All O/17 men the make up.	Ofr.

Army Form C. 2118

WAR DIARY
or
INTELLIGENCE SUMMARY

(Erase heading not required.)

Instructions regarding War Diaries and Intelligence Summaries are contained in F.S. Regs., Part II. and the Staff Manual respectively. Title Pages will be prepared in manuscript.

Place	Date	Hour	Summary of Events and Information	Remarks and references to Appendices
CAMPIGNEULES LES PETITES	14		Three lorries sent out with R Battery. 450 lbs shrapnel, 150 u HE, gunpowder.	Offrs
			1 horse cyclist with pannier for communication with the Division who marched with Division is thus horse shoes. Leave train leaves MONTREUIL at 7.45 pm. Billeting accommodation of this village stated as 6 officers 250 men. 50 horses.	Offrs.
	16		10 Reserve Park wagon teams chalk from MYRON NOTRE DAME thousand to TREPIED stamp.	
"	17		Officers staying for the right on L.of C. report to local commandant officer.	Offrs.

Army Form C. 2118

WAR DIARY
or
INTELLIGENCE SUMMARY
(Erase heading not required.)

Instructions regarding War Diaries and Intelligence Summaries are contained in F.S. Regs., Part II. and the Staff Manual respectively. Title Pages will be prepared in manuscript.

Place	Date	Hour	Summary of Events and Information	Remarks and references to Appendices
CAMPIGNEULES LES PETITES	17		Prevention of foot marks. Oofer the taken. Orphan may be returned or comes who not required at once identified for.	
	18		Very Pink flare immediately in D.I. Queen 2 Paris then the returned to Park.	GRO 2331
	19		Engineers material the purchases by field signature.	GRO 2332
	24		Only 4 those lorries required or cast lectures for the French.	
	25		Some the cast to No 63 Repair shop until congestion at No 1 relieved.	
	26		Tanks in general Hd qrs. Recognised laws necessary.	GRO 2018 2024
	27		Public covers for Vine Hugles. Instructions from Publications Dept. Boulogne. Leave allotment 2 per week from CPWHS	CH

Army Form C. 2118

WAR DIARY
or
INTELLIGENCE SUMMARY
(Erase heading not required.)

Instructions regarding War Diaries and Intelligence Summaries are contained in F. S. Regs., Part II. and the Staff Manual respectively. Title Pages will be prepared in manuscript.

Place.	Date	Hour	Summary of Events and Information	Remarks and references to Appendices
CHAUGNEDLES LES PETITES	28		Divisional Reign completed on lorries.	OM
	29		Total Bonspn. cleared. have Petit proceed vie CALAIS	
			Detail for 8 g. wagons to carry clerk to TREPIED for showering all classes	C C A15/74. 27/10/12.
	30		Certificate made forward for those going on leave to Paris Petrol Consumption for month	
				Mileage	Petrol gallons	mpg.
			Lorries	6134	1121.	5.10.
			Cars	2423	142.	17.76.
			Cycles	1319	33	39.97.

C Manton Capt
G.C.O.M.C.

WAR DIARY
or
INTELLIGENCE SUMMARY

(Erase heading not required.)

Army _____ December 1916

Army Form C. 2118

Place	Date	Hour	Summary of Events and Information	Remarks and references to Appendices
Boulogne	12-12-16		Receipts L.a.a 303 43000	9-12-16 1st Amb/col 8th Inv Div /a.a 303 107000
– do –	21-12-16		– " – 600	29-12-16 do – do – Cardiff Dy 308
– do –	18-12-16		Bristol Dy 16.96	22-12-16 2nd gds Light Am Col Dy Pil 82C 303 6000
– do –	21-12-16		– " –	
Ord Depot	5-12-16		A/a 303 Blank 65.20	6-12-16 2nd Regiments L.a.a 303 (Blank Cart) 10000
			10000	

Vol 24

Confidential
War Diary.
of
3rd Cavalry Ammunition Park.
From 1st January 1917. To 31st January 1917.
(Volume 24)

Army Form C. 2118

WAR DIARY
or
INTELLIGENCE SUMMARY
(Erase heading not required.)

Instructions regarding War Diaries and Intelligence Summaries are contained in F.S. Regs., Part II. and the Staff Manual respectively. Title Pages will be prepared in manuscript.

Place	Date	Hour	Summary of Events and Information	Remarks and references to Appendices
CAMP ICKNIELD LES PETTES	1		Field tactical scheme the Bomb attended gas school for instruction	Clm.
	3		Grenade exercise the drawn from stores last the	Q3Ju
	4		W.O.J.A.I.: Complete course of gas school. Requirements of ammunition to be refitted to Q.E. 15th of each month	F.S.J.u
	7		CPL Bradford attended gas school for course of instruction	CJc
	10		Before a man proceeds on leave to England he must have a certificate to say that he is free from vermin	SCD 5257/26 CJc
	13		Sent NCOs promoted by W.O. Jackson No 18 months continuous service + 6 months in rank of L	CJc arc 1884

WAR DIARY
INTELLIGENCE SUMMARY

Army Form C. 2118

Place	Date	Hour	Summary of Events and Information	Remarks and references to Appendices
CAMPIGNEULES LES PETITES	15		Lethal Machine Gun Fore handed dove grey with black stenciling on future.	HQ 3WD 5665
			Kynoch blank cartridges was working the recoil sufficiently by luking	CPM.
	16		Distinguishing flag for the 3rd br Div. light + dark blue	2nd DG AQ 7/13 CPM.
	17		Left the kation outposk course 9 in gas School. Correspondence received from the ADS+T stating that QMG had noticed as day guard orderlies Sunday 14/7	CPM.
	18		Query received from HQC section regarding WE of bar aur Park.	CPM.

Army Form C. 2118

WAR DIARY
or
INTELLIGENCE SUMMARY
(Erase heading not required.)

Instructions regarding War Diaries and Intelligence Summaries are contained in F. S. Regs., Part II. and the Staff Manual respectively. Title Pages will be prepared in manuscript.

Place	Date	Hour	Summary of Events and Information	Remarks and references to Appendices
PIN RENDEL	19		Inspected MT Books & other helpers unserviceable works. Checked with vendors; found in order.	Gmnt. Cm.
"	20		Cases entrusted by Military Police. Cars examined & all with seriously reasons the outskirts of origin. Three undocked found same sterilization fuel.	DRO 2362 Offr. Clr.
"	21		Imprest Account number allotted SAcc 1003	Staff Payments
"	22		Hours inspected workshops. Day guard the mounted. Incoming guard started for 24 hrs duty in place of 12 hrs as before.	Offr. GRO 2090
"	24		1/3 under upper surface of lookout plan of handle flank fines. Saw the taken in motor lines near a building.	Offr. 2091 Gdn.

WAR DIARY
or
INTELLIGENCE SUMMARY
(Erase heading not required.)

Army Form C. 2118

Place	Date	Hour	Summary of Events and Information	Remarks and references to Appendices
CAMP BAZECOLA LES PETITES	26		In the event of a Raw Reserve Park before the end of rations &c	O.C.R.C. Offr.
	27		Care of MT Vehicles. Overloading " " " have tonnes	Apr 1907 2nd none 118
	28		Individuals received for commission in the Artillery. Inspection for alteration in WE asked for. Answered. i No gunner officer ii Sorry for explosives.	Offr.
	29		Nominal roll of gunners sufficiently young were to send back their transfer to Battery & been desirable	Arc 1912 Offr.

1875 Wt. W593/826 1,000,000 4/15 J.B.C. & A. A.D.S.S./Forms/C. 2118.

Army Form C. 2118

WAR DIARY
or
INTELLIGENCE SUMMARY
(Erase heading not required.)

Instructions regarding War Diaries and Intelligence Summaries are contained in F.S. Regs., Part II. and the Staff Manual respectively. Title Pages will be prepared in manuscript.

Place	Date	Hour	Summary of Events and Information	Remarks and references to Appendices
CAMPAGNOLES LES PETITES	Feb 30		Rem Sergt RITA suitable for Squadron gas NCO	DGO.
			Lt Lyttle observed Lewis gun school for commission	
			Authority received for making two NCO's workshop i/e 1 Sgt & 1 Cpl	GHQ
	"	31	Method of carrying out F.N.O.1.	1105/8MB
			Venereal disease. No case for period Officers NCO & men	223'/(Reg)
			Mileage & Petrol consumption for month	B/S466
			Miles Gals MPG	GHQ
			Lorries 2225 365 6.09	GHQ
			Cars 2456 146 17.02	
			Cycles 1959 51 38.41	

Vol 25

Confidential
War Diary
of
3rd Cavalry Ammunition Park.
From 1st February 1917. To 28th February 1917.

(Volume 25)

WAR DIARY
or
INTELLIGENCE SUMMARY
(Erase heading not required.)

Army Form C.2118

Instructions regarding War Diaries and Intelligence Summaries are contained in F.S. Regs, Part II. and the Staff Manual respectively. Title Pages will be prepared in manuscript.

Place	Date	Hour	Summary of Events and Information	Remarks and references to Appendices
CAMPIGNEULES LES PETITES				
February	1		Class 'A' M.T. Drivers will accept no reinforcements. These men showed to trained as M.T drivers by units.	Doy 189. Gpn.
	2		Medal Rolls. Nominal Rolls the body of all men serving with units.	CO 1 the Green 197.
	3		Training of parties for the accomodation of books are carried out by Brand Regimental Office	Clk. Aro 1931.
			Medical Officer carrying out innoculation showed make return in AB 64.	C.C. A 1862.
	4		Daily return of lorries off the road the short the off.	Aro 1938.
	5		Seen the supported with Tarens nor Chin Chain he thought told or to find for Drivers 4 hours for motor tyres available during	Gpn Gpn

1875 Wt. W 593/826 1,000,000 4/15 J.B.C. & A. A.D.S.S./Forms/C. 2118.

WAR DIARY or INTELLIGENCE SUMMARY

Place	Date	Hour	Summary of Events and Information	Remarks and references to Appendices
CAMPIGNEULES LES PETITES	6.		Proposal of office moved as per FSR Pt II Ch 16 § 129 para 2.	ACI 1939.
	7.		AFG 1098 is no authority for establishments	DRO 107.
			Guard to be told off today as well as at night.	ACI 1894.
			Orders received for men relieved for inoculation	
	8.		Ten of Lewis gun & motor car Ambulances. Found in order. Workshops officer given copy.	Dy Or 190.
			Classification of MT personnel in AF B 64 to be completed	OC Coy
	9.		Leave stopped except for those entitled pgs. by mail boat	
	10.		PMC. visited lines. Oil stores found smoking wires on two lorries. Order issued prohibiting this as a dangerous practice.	Ch.

WAR DIARY
or
INTELLIGENCE SUMMARY
(Erase heading not required.)

Army Form C. 2118

Instructions regarding War Diaries and Intelligence Summaries are contained in F.S. Regs., Part II. and the Staff Manual respectively. Title Pages will be prepared in manuscript.

Place	Date	Hour	Summary of Events and Information	Remarks and references to Appendices
CAMIGNEULES LES PETITES.	11.		Boards the Motor Vehicle Chassis with numbers of mobilisation were assembled. Reinforcements having still not knowledge should be possible in view that their many specify. Started a door for photography Ray.	ADC 1879. GM.
			Triumph Cycle Frame No 255050 } Examined DTC Engine No. 35723 }	GM. ASC CO 14.
			Return submitted for new machine.	
"	12		War Diaries should conflict as possible. Difficulty in obtaining supplies of medicine totes whaler. Cretes that Kraft Teresa Sweetas Chocks. Generated the Cases taken	

Army Form C. 2118

WAR DIARY
or
INTELLIGENCE SUMMARY
(Erase heading not required.)

Instructions regarding War Diaries and Intelligence Summaries are contained in F.S. Regs., Part II. and the Staff Manual respectively. Title Pages will be prepared in manuscript.

Place	Date	Hour	Summary of Events and Information	Remarks and references to Appendices
CAMP DE NEUFCHÂTEL PETITES	12.		Recd. requisn. for men who have served in apprenticeshp as artificers.	Offr.
	13.		Arrangements for a forward move received from Q. at 11.15 p.m. Stores to be collected under charge of one man. Units of the Coln. to entrain their stores. Return to be rendered.	Offr. MgGr 5840.
	14		Recd. 67 men who enlisted at W.H.T. after 10th Nov. 1915 to be sent to O/C Arc Section H.Q's Office Base. Such men in future to come under ordinary rules of Regy.	BOC Sec. HQ Base. OComc. Qmaster.
	15		Ref: Oil stoves in tents. Notices to be posted in each tent.	
	16.		Notices on stoves all posted.	Offr.

WAR DIARY
or
INTELLIGENCE SUMMARY

(Erase heading not required.)

Army Form C. 2118

Place	Date	Hour	Summary of Events and Information	Remarks and references to Appendices
CAMPBELLTOWN & TENBY	18		Men arrived following repaired for holy Cycle but has been type to visit to inspection of any two wing squadron [Inchmurray].	Apx.
			To Scorpion Carter only one tenant the sea in [Eng.]	Apx.
			Lec 6t. Hume in Bedford Caunter re	Apx P.137.
	19		lonie at advance on its road during low [tide].	Ocean Apx.
			2 Spearman Test used for driving actors of Pan 2. Ri-arms. Recut at Mr. B. R.P. detached & also of Spearman & action of lonie to action system every started inspection of lonies.	Apx.
			Tuesday at 12.p.m. Report [remains] Nicholson followed Wednesday.	Apx.
	20		Patrol boats sent in for all cases of damage. Estimated cost of class parts to be included.	Apx. Apx 1948.

Army Form C.2118

WAR DIARY
or
INTELLIGENCE SUMMARY

(Erase heading not required.)

Place	Date	Hour	Summary of Events and Information	Remarks and references to Appendices
CANPICNULES LES PETITES	27		Forms transit application forwarded OC.AIC in case of the Major J. Charged with Otterburgford Stationary of a Casuarine. (ie Mr Field Boots).	CM OC ASC GM.
"		22	Instruction to be given BMT details in construction of vehicles on the weight information. Return card stating that no vehicles need to evacuate as immobile.	CM.
"	28	23	Forwarded letters to be sealed up in the presence of an officer. Regards S/contemps for Cartridge lamps loved to Labaed Type Press KLYS OC	2CD 5646/1 FAR 8137 GM.

A.D.S.S./Forms/C. 2118.

WAR DIARY
or
INTELLIGENCE SUMMARY
(Erase heading not required.)

Army Form C. 2118

Place	Date	Hour	Summary of Events and Information	Remarks and references to Appendices
CHAMPIEN/SOULT LES PETITES.	24		Sgt Chapple ACC attend gas school from 19th Feb - 23rd Feb; and is suitable as Operator gas NCO.	A.G.O. 2nd Opn.
	25		Consumption of Petrol. Note GRO 317, v.III. Consumption of Petrol in store to be investigated. Enquiry to be made into excessive consumption and the officer concerned about recent his initials.	Opn. MDSVy c/193 Opn.
	26		Observer returned for MRFC. Some of lectures started on hot Reading Driving Orders. L.D.O. instruction. Examination on each subject being held & new classified according trades obtained.	Opn.

Army Form C. 2118

WAR DIARY
or
INTELLIGENCE SUMMARY

(Erase heading not required.)

Instructions regarding War Diaries and Intelligence Summaries are contained in F. S. Regs., Part II. and the Staff Manual respectively. Title Pages will be prepared in manuscript.

Place	Date	Hour	Summary of Events and Information	Remarks and references to Appendices
CAMBLIGNEUL WOOD TENTES	27		Return of lorries hired the seven or less day of each month.	Appx.
"	28		All motor cycle totals to be worked out number of cycle. Any for the said for.	Appx.
			Nil return of recommendations for military honour.	Appx 2010.
			Return of mileage & Petrol consumption & MPG for the month	
			Miles Petrol galls. M.P.G. Lorries 2146 351 6.11 Cars 1786 99 18.05 Cycles 1645 41 40.12	
				A.J.Martin Capt OC Troops A.D. 2/3/17

1875 Wt. W593/826 1,000,000 4/15 J.B.C. & A. A.D.S.S./Forms/C. 2118.

WAR DIARY
or
INTELLIGENCE SUMMARY

Army Form C.2118

(Erase heading not required.)

.... February 1917 2nd Bn Am Cav ....

Place	Date	Hour	Summary of Events and Information	Remarks and references to Appendices
	13-2-17	8 AM 10 PM	Receipts	
	14-2-17	3 PM 10.30 PM	A.T.O. Am Goyt	
			R.U.A. – 303 Roll	
				880
			10-2-17 A.T.O. Am Goyt	120
			14-2-17 A.T.O. A.P.R.	272
			15-2-17 S.F. — no —	2008
			16-2-17 S.A.A. 303 Ball — 8.30	2601
			17-2-17 — no — 20	2161
			18-2-17 — 20 —	2207
			19-2-17 — 20 —	
			3-2-17 Grenades rifle 1005	144

Vol 26

Confidential
War Diary
of
3rd Cavalry Ammunition Park.

from 1st March 1917 to March 31st 1917.

(Volume 26)

Army Form C. 2118

WAR DIARY
or
INTELLIGENCE SUMMARY
(Erase heading not required.)

Instructions regarding War Diaries and Intelligence Summaries are contained in F. S. Regs., Part II. and the Staff Manual respectively. Title Pages will be prepared in manuscript.

Place	Date	Hour	Summary of Events and Information	Remarks and references to Appendices
CAMP DNCLES LES PETITES	MARCH 1		Received Standard "Tool Kits for Lorries". Similar kits to be kept in Cab down in log book.	AF 2113 Ofm. AFG 2908 Ofm
	2		Correspondence on man power received. State made out & forward. Got men from 30-40 coast depot for necessary duties.	Ofm
	3		Workshop totals now compiled according to establishment.	Ofm
	4		Lieut Howard are proceeded to England for Commission in RGA. Returning correspondence received from Dy T. concerning care of MT vehicles. These should be noted & taken as may a possible Case of Casualties.	Ofm Ofm
	5		Return of Parking Cards DMT Depots. As may as possible unserviceable articles may be returned in these cases.	DOT CPL 14 SA Ofm

1875 Wt. W593/826 1,000,000 4/15 J.B.C. & A. A.D.S.S./Forms/C. 2118.

Army Form C. 2118

WAR DIARY
or
INTELLIGENCE SUMMARY

(Erase heading not required.)

Instructions regarding War Diaries and Intelligence Summaries are contained in F. S. Regs., Part II. and the Staff Manual respectively. Title Pages will be prepared in manuscript.

Place	Date	Hour	Summary of Events and Information	Remarks and references to Appendices
CAMPIGNEULLES LES PETITES.	5.		Chassis No. of the vehicle for which stores are required should on demand.	App. 2012.
"	6		No. 101 types of Ervick machine marked z/z and for time should be retained on inventories. This applies also to all & upwards. If its lot needs to have out, that as necessary.	App. 2023. CFM
"	7		Stations officers in future will render Defective Report with Services Rept in October. WO will await materials supplies to Army return from the Station offices before it is the army.	CFM
"	8		The practice of starting engines by means of towing with cars / or in second gear to engage unsuccinct. Steps should only the engaged.	Soft Cy 801. CFM

1875 Wt. W593/826 1,000,000 4/15 J.B.C. & A. A.D.S.S./Forms/C. 2118.

Army Form C. 2118

WAR DIARY
or
INTELLIGENCE SUMMARY
(Erase heading not required.)

Instructions regarding War Diaries and Intelligence Summaries are contained in F.S. Regs., Part II. and the Staff Manual respectively. Title Pages will be prepared in manuscript.

Place	Date	Hour	Summary of Events and Information	Remarks and references to Appendices
CAMP PICQUIGNY LES PETITES	10		Men endeavour in case of emergency defeat to hidden centre. Chiefs of information the attaches to have warrants.	Offr. June 2045.
"	11		Lunatics afflicting one officio stand to appear until AQMG. QMG instead of QMG.	Ane 2045 CM.
"	12		Every Endeavour to be care to where use the boundaries with T.A.B. One year from previous TV inoculation to be accepted as a standard.	EU
"	13			2 CD
"	14		Nota custodished D.V.C.F.A. of inoculation.	3 CD 6043.
"	15		Scale of Rations. 1 Part 3 cattle every 10 camels 1 Pean, 10 " 1 Zite had Pramus " 10 "	Ane 2000

1875 Wt. W593/826 1,000,000 4/15 J.B.C. & A. A.D.S.S./Forms/C. 2118.

WAR DIARY
or
INTELLIGENCE SUMMARY

(Erase heading not required.)

Army Form C. 2118

Place	Date	Hour	Summary of Events and Information	Remarks and references to Appendices
CHIPICFOLES AZK PETITES.	15		DBRs the field Egan offices. Nosies & Armstrong held on Lifton down on Carrigan.	Arc/2058. Arc/1839.
			Dump blocked vehicle at TREPIED. 200+ N of I	"
	16		SAA marked K.N 1915 MK VII & G 15" HV not to be used in future	(Jun Q3d)
			DBRs the Silver March 31st	Qm.
	17		Indent submitted for DBRs. 20 trys & 20 drums amended. NSM Alexander interviewed by G.O.C. for Commission in A.P.C. Left today for Paris. Pte Park returned to BEAURAINVILLE. Detachment of 5th Bn.	Qm.
	18		Claim for stores re settled by Claims Office. No further applicants for commissions or service with Heavy Branch Machine Gun Corps received.	Qm. Qm.

WAR DIARY
or
INTELLIGENCE SUMMARY

Army Form C. 2118

Place	Date	Hour	Summary of Events and Information	Remarks and references to Appendices
CAMPNEUF LES PETITES	20		Lt Grutchfield A O D arrived Dumped Chapel 18hrs/Eyes	Offr
"	21		Established 7 Batteries	
			GC Arty forming PL 180	
			103 in lieu of 910 ring	
			Area 9 6 hrs	
			GC McClasper Pd 158 any 6 in times care: 144	
			Detonators No 8 in tins of 26: 225	
			Fuze inst. in drums of 100 + 300 +	
			Dets No 11 in tins of I Jet Thomo 72 fuze	
			hatches Parrien a hur 913 234	
			Grenades hill No 5 1800	Q 3 e D.
			Walk	Offr
"	22		Received 1 Water thank ptrailer from Status at T Bty Péconne	Offr

Army Form C. 2118.

WAR DIARY
or
INTELLIGENCE SUMMARY.
(Erase heading not required.)

Instructions regarding War Diaries and Intelligence Summaries are contained in F. S. Regs., Part II. and the Staff Manual respectively. Title pages will be prepared in manuscript.

Place	Date	Hour	Summary of Events and Information	Remarks and references to Appendices
CAMP'GNEULES LES PETITES	23		Officers went the transport & some more classis to with without authority of ADST.	ACI 2090.
			When lorries are required from column in reply of AgnC of MT Vehicle the correspondence and other officer papers should contain a statement that the necessary entry has been made in AB64.	ACI 2091.
	24		1 NCO & 3 Gunners returned store in place of forces men. The only lorries now accepted by the Grand Parc are Bouche Farning. Car Laurer or Pink Peerles. Summer Time adopted.	GRO 2416. GRO 148.
	25		32 officers & rounds N. in Park to be returned Aff Div. 491 as Division including N will	Gw.
	26		ABD's the first to join by April 3rd. PH lehivels Tank-jar jiggle the returned place	Q 307 CRO 51 gm.

T2134. Wt. W708-776. 500000. 4/15. Sir J. C. & S.

Army Form C. 2118.

WAR DIARY
or
INTELLIGENCE SUMMARY.
(Erase heading not required.)

Instructions regarding War Diaries and Intelligence Summaries are contained in F.S. Regs., Part II. and the Staff Manual respectively. Title pages will be prepared in manuscript.

Place	Date	Hour	Summary of Events and Information	Remarks and references to Appendices
CAMPIGNEULES LES PETITES	27		Defective rounds of S.N. ammunition returned Base. Les Landes leave. Veh. Sect. returned to Pernes.	GM
	28		1 Limber of G.S. Wagon arrived for repair. 6 limbers returned repaired to 7th Bde.	GM
	29		14 men mobiles via T.M.B. Board sat on units Clothing, unserviceable store wasted report. On 7th returned Rail Head.	GM
	30		Discharge of Gas Carts. Picric Park played the up D.	GM
	31		Adm received for Capt Newton to report for duty to S. Corps Ammunition Park for duty. O.May 0. Blanchet A.S.C. asked duty commencing of 3rd Jan. Ammn Park	GM

WAR DIARY
or
INTELLIGENCE SUMMARY.
(Erase heading not required.)

Army Form C. 2118.

Place	Date	Hour	Summary of Events and Information	Remarks and references to Appendices
CHAPIGNEOLE S LES PETITES	31.		Mileage & Petrol Consumption for March. Miles Petrol/galls. MPG. Lorries 4066 699 5.81. Cars 1836 78. 23.53. Cycles 1648 41. 40.19. Afunonto Capt Park OC 3rd Army Park 4/17.	

Army Form C. 2118

WAR DIARY
or
INTELLIGENCE SUMMARY.

(Erase heading not required.) Army [?] March 1917

Instructions regarding War Diaries and Intelligence Summaries are contained in F. S. Regs., Part II. and the Staff Manual respectively. Title pages will be prepared in manuscript.

Place	Date	Hour	Summary of Events and Information	Remarks and references to Appendices
Receipts				
10-3-17	Q.F.13pr Shrapnel	O.C. Festin 580	10-3-17 Q.F.13pr Shrapnel O.C. 4th 13th Am Col	346
22-3-17	— do —	O.C. Dannes 1224	22-3-17 — do —	792
27-3-17	— do —	O.C. 13pr Pkr 83	27-3-17 — do — O.C. 13pr Pkr	83
27-3-17	— do —	O.C. Dannes 492	27-3-17 — do — O.C. Boulogne	32
26-3-17	— do —	O.C. 4th Bde Am Col 376	27-3-17 — do — O.C. Boulogne	376
10-3-17	8.F.13pr H.E.	O.C. Festin 120	10-3-17 — do — H.E. O.C. 4th Bde Am Col	262
20-3-17	— do —	— — 8	20-3-17 — do —	8
22-3-17	— do —	O.C. Dannes 344	22-3-17 — do — O.C. Boulogne	8
22-3-17	— do —	O.C. Boulogne 8	23-3-17 — do — O.C. 4th Bde Am Col	1
26-3-17	8pm O.F.	O.C. — do — 76		

Vol 27

Confidential
War Diary
of
3rd Cavalry Ammunition Park
From 1st April 1917 to 30th April 1917
(Volume 27)

Army Form C. 2118.

WAR DIARY
or
INTELLIGENCE SUMMARY.
(Erase heading not required.)

Place	Date	Hour	Summary of Events and Information	Remarks and references to Appendices
CAMBLIGNEUL	APRIL			
PETITES.	1.		Maps of German positions in front of ARRAS received. Also Orders for the Control of Traffic leading through ARRAS during operations will west of ARRAS town.	Offr. 3rd Army Offr.
"	2.		Line of M.T. by civilians to cease. Bapaume closed for Red 1 Movement from Balance 110.29th 1830	HQ Offr.
"	3.		All ADP's filled slightly in Lachrymatory gas. Billeting in army area there are other various ad area commands. No will be occupied without reference to these officers.	Offr.
"	4.		Strenuous duty return no longer required. Movement order received.	Offr.

WAR DIARY
or
INTELLIGENCE SUMMARY.

Army Form C. 2118.

Place	Date	Hour	Summary of Events and Information	Remarks and references to Appendices
CAMPAGNE LES PETITES	5.		Move 67 mile N.J. PREVENT followed for 26 hours.	Ocean. Offr.
"	6.		All Claims settled. Particular attention the paid to march discipline	Acc
LA BRIQUETERIE	7.		Moved to LABRIQ VETERIE 1 mile N.of PREVENT. Route taken MONTREUIL HESDIN. ST-POL. Started & inspected 5.30 p.m. Attended conference at office of O.C. ese at BOUBERS & received orders to hand over all ammunition to A Cecilian H.T. Coy. 3rd Cav. Div.	2/11/17. Offr.
LEVY SR FLOCIEL	8.		Stonis dumped ammunition. Picked up 12 OR of Offrs & transferred from to GOUY-EN-ARTOIS. Handed over ammunition to Capt Bulle O/C 1/c A.H.T. Coy. Halted 10 A.M. finished 12.30 p.m. Proceeded to LEVY BERLETTE & having halted will ammunition returned to Locality on main ARRAS-ST POL road of halts & CAV. Divl Corps for orders. St FLOCIEL station. Last lorry halted at 1.8 p.m.	Offr.

Army Form C. 2118.

WAR DIARY
or
INTELLIGENCE SUMMARY.
(Erase heading not required.)

Instructions regarding War Diaries and Intelligence Summaries are contained in F.S. Regs., Part II. and the Staff Manual respectively. Title pages will be prepared in manuscript.

Place	Date	Hour	Summary of Events and Information	Remarks and references to Appendices
LIGHT ST FLOCHEL	9.		Ration collected from R.S.O. LIGNY ST FLOCHEL station. Workshop Hutted in AVERDOIGNE.	
"	10.		Major Blundell O.C. arrived from 8 Corps Sigs Park & takes over command of 30 Car Amm Park.	
"	11		Major J.H. Blundell R.S.C. took over command from Capt C.J. Merlin R.S.C.	
"	12"		Capt C.J. Merlin R.S.C. proceeded before on L.T. on re-assumed to "J" Corps Ammunit Parks. R.Q.M.S. G.I. Q.G.H.O. A.D.S.& T. Au Corps & Lt. R.S.C. 3" Cav Div returned to duty & arrived & Major J.H. Blundell R.S.C. and departure of Capt C.J. Merlin M.C. R.S.C. Ration collected from R.S.O. LIGNY ST FLOCHEL Statii 2 Empty lorries 6 lorries J.R.R.dumped 65 tons & cart and horse for S.S.O. 3"Cav Div	

T2134. Wt. W708—776. 500000. 4/15. Sir J. C. & S.

Place	Date	Hour	Summary of Events and Information	Remarks and references to Appendices
LIGNY ST. FLOCHEL	12th	6 a.m.	Shrapnel dumped to Convoy charged to Cavalry from ARRAS to GOOY (Lieut. Ashwin returning 1.15 a.m. artillery repairs.) M5/4970 Pte (9599pr) 1x56EY R.H. Delivered to 3rd Armd. T. R.F.C. Lily Views to Cavanieur.	
	13th		Lorry No. 10836 Halford belonging to 3rd Car Div Supply Col with MCC 64 H.Bau charging R.E. Stores issued by Q.M.G. Car Corps to remain at 3rd Car Amm Park until further orders. Four Lorries ordered to report to O/C Cav Div Ammunition Park – ARRAS to be prepared to clear up the battlefield below ARRAS & MONCHY LE-PREUX.	
	14th		Two lorries loaded with H.E. and Shrapnel to French Art. at GOOY then to Cav. Ammn Park dump ARRAS, unloaded and returned to Park. M2/082036 Pte MARSDEN, A.J. Delivered by an officer of 15 R.F.C. at DOULLENS Lily & Views for Conveyance to the R.F.C.	

WAR DIARY or INTELLIGENCE SUMMARY.

Army Form C. 2118.

Place	Date	Hour	Summary of Events and Information	Remarks and references to Appendices
LIGNY ST FLOCHEL	15"	5 a.m.	Convoyed Ordnance went to Div. Troops at 2nd Bde 1st Cav Div from LIGNY ST FLOCHEL Station, after dumping ordered 2nd & Reserve to 3rd Cav Div Supply Col at dump.	
		3 a.m.	to BLAVINCOURT to turn over to 3rd Cav Div Supply Col. after ten days to 3rd Cav Div Supply Col. All ammunition & two dumps in Park. Addn Cav Corps. Q 2231.	
		3 a.m.	proceeded to 3rd Cav Div Place H.T Coy at ESTREE- MURRIN 65 feet of ammunition and into to Cav Corps dump ARRAS	
"	16"	3 a.m.	departed to RUE FOSSEUX - BARLY to Pouit of kms refs of 2nd Life Guards, an officer reported to "B" DIV HQ for orders.	
		1 hour collected supplies, ammunition and supplies from C. Bty RHA and returned to rail head		
		Then to GOUY aux River 3 Envies 16" to FOSSEUX to hew elements then as & kms refs to 5th Bde to FRONTEN-LÉ-GRAND.		
"	17"			

Army Form C. 2118.

WAR DIARY
or
INTELLIGENCE SUMMARY.
(Erase heading not required.)

Instructions regarding War Diaries and Intelligence
Summaries are contained in F. S. Regs., Part II.
and the Staff Manual respectively. Title pages
will be prepared in manuscript.

Place	Date	Hour	Summary of Events and Information	Remarks and references to Appendices
LIGNY-ST-FLOCHEL	18th		Shown proceeded to Amm dump Div⁹ to ARRAS to try and change for 13 Pdr. C. & 3 Pdr and have to send back. Ammn proceeded with'y. OCC OC HQ⁵ to report to mechanic to Puff-type 8" Bde. Ration carried to CC 19t⁸	
"	19"		PARK moved to REGNAUVILLE with one lorry. Moved to lose charged with one officer at all R.F.A. parades. All lorries were in elcty trains order to return home park.	
REGNAUVILLE	20"		Two horse lorries to ROO BOUQ MAISON R. & SE Empfield - diels/stn. 19 lorries to report to O.T. Cav Reinforcement Camp FREVENT to convey bags of charcoal ammn to 8th Bde to blubby ann.	
"	21st		21 lorries to FREVENT to clear'g as in 20th. 1 lorry to Lys p.m. at St.POL afterwards to ONE Park Ships Lonet rcle Ammunition to return.	

T2134. Wt. W708-776. 500000. 4/15. Sir J. C. & S.

Army Form C. 2118.

WAR DIARY
or
INTELLIGENCE SUMMARY.
(Erase heading not required.)

Instructions regarding War Diaries and Intelligence Summaries are contained in F. S. Regs., Part II. and the Staff Manual respectively. Title pages will be prepared in manuscript.

Place	Date	Hour	Summary of Events and Information	Remarks and references to Appendices
REGNAUVILLE	22nd		One lorry detailed to Rly. report at Staging at 8.0 a.m. on G.S. duty	
		23rd	to C.T. Cav. Div Ammunition Park, ARRAS, for one day duty	
		4 lorries	to MARESQUEL and report to Staff Capt. 6th Bde. Stores Distribution	
		3 lorries	to ABBEVILLE on entraining duty	
		4 "	" BOUQUEMAISON " "	
		3 "	to Rest Stations to bring ammunition to Rail Park	
		1 "	to lift from St. POL. Shells to Rest Stns. ammun. around Stanley and return	
	23rd	2 lorries	to DOURIER to carry India troops from 7th Bde.	
		11 lorries	to BEAUDRAINVILLE. Stores sent to S.S.O.	
		4 "	to Rest Stations to bring Ammn. to Rail Park	
	24th	1 lorry	to 2 park to distribute aeroplane escort to aerodromes	
		1 "	to TREPIED to clear Stores and deliver to Div H.Q.	
		1 "	to LIGNY-ST-FLOCHEL to Clear Unit to Div. H.Q.	

Army Form C. 2118.

WAR DIARY
or
INTELLIGENCE SUMMARY.
(Erase heading not required.)

Place	Date	Hour	Summary of Events and Information	Remarks and references to Appendices
REGNAUVILLE	24		1 Coy. Cyclists amounts to various regiments of the Div.	
			2 Coy. detachment arrive at Thurs to Recce Cd at VIRONCHAUX.	
			1 " to HESDIN to S.O.G.Hq. conveying & fetching Ord. at about 6"	
			to Div.	
			1 " to BERCK to return bicycles to O.T.R.S.C. Div.	
"	25"		1 Coy. to Advance Party of Main Corps FONTAINE-SUR-MAYE and late	
			6" Base Recce. depot at ECHINGHEN.	
			1 Coy. attached amounts to various regiments	
"	26"		Few Coys. to Freyer Street & also to Royal Horse Guards.	
"	26"		1 Coy. to NAMBRIS-St-MARTIN with amounts	
"	27"		14 Coy. to BOUQMAISON conveying with supplies at about 15pack	
"			1 " to LIGESCOURT to Aux. H.T. Coy.	

WAR DIARY
or
INTELLIGENCE SUMMARY.
(Erase heading not required.)

Army Form C. 2118.

Place	Date	Hour	Summary of Events and Information	Remarks and references to Appendices
REGNAUVILLE	28th		1 Army sent to Col at VIRONCHAUX.	
			3 " Offrs to 2d Brigade dump	
			2 " " " 6 Div dump dump	
			1 " " " 3rd Dragoon Guards as C.Nco.	
			1 " " " 1st Royal Dragoons	
			1 " " " New Zealand Company	
			1 " " " 6" Howitzer Section	
			7 " " " BEAURAINVILLE to S.O.	
"	29th		No 265 2036 Pte MARSDEN. A.J. proceeded on dy to RFC Carlstone Depot.	
"	30th		Car M1612 conveyed 2nd Lieuts 6" & 3rd DAC Repair Shop.	
			14 buns to BOUQMAISON Falleu out.	
			Pte sent the infantry beamn of become to 2nd Car Coys allied 1st CD/M.	
			1 Army to Army Col with convoi	
			1 " to RENTY for 1st 155 R.P.A. Sleigh 123 Repaired Cooper 2 Saxon	

Army Form C. 2118

WAR DIARY
or
INTELLIGENCE SUMMARY
(Erase heading not required.)

Instructions regarding War Diaries and Intelligence Summaries are contained in F. S. Regs., Part II. and the Staff Manual respectively. Title Pages will be prepared in manuscript.

Place	Date	Hour	Summary of Events and Information	Remarks and references to Appendices
			Mileage & Petrol Consumption for Chart.	
			Miles Petrol (Gals) Miles per Gal.	
			Lorries 11640 2144 5.54	
			Cars 3295 146 18.4	
			Cycles 1635 14 31.38	

10/5/17

Army Form C. 2118.

WAR DIARY
or
INTELLIGENCE SUMMARY.
(Erase heading not required.)

Ammunition April 1917

Instructions regarding War Diaries and Intelligence Summaries are contained in F. S. Regs., Part II. and the Staff Manual respectively. Title pages will be prepared in manuscript.

Place	Date	Hour	Summary of Events and Information	Remarks and references to Appendices
		Receipt	Issues	
	6-4-17	Army A.T. 13 pr Shrapnel 1756	6-4-17 A.T.V Bry 3rd Can Div 24 13 pr Shrapnel 2024	
	23-4-17	A.H. Bry 3 Can Div — 20 — 2024	26-4-17 DC Amn Col 3rd Can Div — 1 —	1
	28-4-17	Amn Col — 1 — 1	— do — "K" Bty Raa — 1 —	5
	— do —	"K" Bty Raa — 20 —	8-4-17 a.H. Bry 3rd Can Div H.E.	676
	— do —	— do — H.E. 57	26-4-17 Amn Col 2" — 1 —	2
	8-4-17	Loddy A.T. 13 pr H.E. 948	— do — "K" Bty Raa	2
	28-4-17	A.H. Bry 3rd Can Div — do — 676	24-4-17 H.A. 2.H. V.Bry 3rd Can Div 18pdr 303	683.14
	28-4-17	Amn Col 3rd Can Div — do — 2	H.A.	115.000
	— do —	"K" Bty Raa — do — 2	3 pr A.P. E	110
	28-4-17	A.H. Bry 3rd Can Div I.R.A. 105,000	11-4-17 DC Amn Col 3rd Can Div T.R.a	101,000
	11.4.17	Army 3 pr A.P. E 110	27.4.17 — do — N.S Cyes	2000
			26-4-17 Amn Col 3rd Can Div 12a	15.000
			9-4-17 — do — do — 12a	6.000
			27-4-17 Royal Horse Guards 12a	10,000
			30-4-17 DC Amn Col 3rd Can Div 12a	22.000
			— do — Smoke	552
	30.4.17	— 1 —	Mark III am 1"	150

Vol 28

Confidential

War Diary

of

3rd Cavalry Ammunition Park

From 1st May 1917 to 31st May 1917.

(Volume 28)

Army Form C. 2118.

WAR DIARY
of
INTELLIGENCE SUMMARY.
(Erase heading not required.)

Instructions regarding War Diaries and Intelligence Summaries are contained in F. S. Regs., Part II. and the Staff Manual respectively. Title pages will be prepared in manuscript.

Place	Date	Hour	Summary of Events and Information	Remarks and references to Appendices
REGNAUVILLE	1st May		1 Army Wll Armoured Car Sqn Kennard.	
"	2nd		12 Coni Recons to ESTREES-LES-CRECY.	
"	3rd		1 Army to Div HQ. Receiving orders from TREPIED.	
			1 " Wll Armoured C to 3rd Dragoon Guards.	
"	4th		Coopers passed by Road circulating to another fancy ndings. 1 Army to 3rd Field Squadron R.E.S.	
"	5th		nil	
"	6th		1 Army to Wjn Them Fd Pol.	
"			1 " Wll Armoured to Armn Col and Pochniform Squadron.	

T2134. Wt. W708—776. 500000. 4/15. Sir J. C. & S.

Army Form C. 2118.

WAR DIARY
or
INTELLIGENCE SUMMARY.
(Erase heading not required.)

Instructions regarding War Diaries and Intelligence Summaries are contained in F. S. Regs., Part II. and the Staff Manual respectively. Title pages will be prepared in manuscript.

Place	Date	Hour	Summary of Events and Information	Remarks and references to Appendices
RÉGNAUVILLE	8 "		nil	
"	9 "		nil	
"	10 "		Powers telegrams to Aux 1st Co ordered on return enrte to hand over	
"	11 "	6 o'clock	to 7th Bn. & return the to HQ dump ex RANG-DU-FLIERS	
		11 "	" returns AUX HQ Co Powers to railhead at DANNES.	
		1 "	" return & amm to 8"/13th Machine Gun section	
"	12 "	5 hours	to VRON, then to ROUSSENT to carry into to BEAURAINVILLE	
		6 "	" SAULCHOY, ARGOULES & PREAUX Branch posts "	
		2 "	" MAINTENAY "	
"	13 "	1 lorry expected to Q to chts	
		16 "	" 3" Cow Supply Col to chts as return up to Regn 13 "	

Army Form C. 2118.

WAR DIARY
or
INTELLIGENCE SUMMARY.
(Erase heading not required.)

Instructions regarding War Diaries and Intelligence Summaries are contained in F. S. Regs., Part II. and the Staff Manual respectively. Title pages will be prepared in manuscript.

Place	Date	Hour	Summary of Events and Information	Remarks and references to Appendices
RÉGNAUVILLE	14th		Car No. M 29565 (MAXWELL) joined from Car Cops. Troops happy etc.	
"	15th		did	
"	16th		1 lorry to by 2 Run St Pol.	
"	17th		Armr. car loaded on train went to Co to move.	
"	18th		Company left for VILLERS-BOCAGE. Two cars sent to Tyne Pans DOULLENS.	
VILLERS-BOCAGE	19th		Company left for VILLERS CARBONNEL.	
VILLERS CARBONNEL	20th		3 lorries changed camm and reported to Town Major in PÉRONNE Brady M.G.	
"	21st		Company left for TINCOURT.	

Army Form C. 2118.

WAR DIARY
or
INTELLIGENCE SUMMARY.
(Erase heading not required.)

Instructions regarding War Diaries and Intelligence Summaries are contained in F. S. Regs., Part II. and the Staff Manual respectively. Title pages will be prepared in manuscript.

Place	Date	Hour	Summary of Events and Information	Remarks and references to Appendices
TINCOURT	22nd		nil	
"	23rd		Lorries to LA FLAQUE, R.E. dump to 32 German prisoners at an Adrian hut at dump at ROSIÈL.	
"	24th		4 lorries steel fatigue at ROISSEL.	
			1 " to 39 C.C.S. TINCOURT, to repair electric light public railway.	
			2 " to Type from PÉRONNE	
			5 " to MONTIGNY now linked to TINCOURT for R.E.s	
			1 " " Le QUINCONCE Allied Company from 2nd Corps Ammu Park.	
"	25th		1 lorry to BOUZLY in field fatigue	
"	26th		19 lorries to + 10 Portland at Corined Ammn to ARPs at VILLERS FAUCON at HANCOURT.	

WAR DIARY
or
INTELLIGENCE SUMMARY

(Erase heading not required.)

Army Form C. 2118

Instructions regarding War Diaries and Intelligence Summaries are contained in F. S. Regs., Part II. and the Staff Manual respectively. Title Pages will be prepared in manuscript.

Place	Date	Hour	Summary of Events and Information	Remarks and references to Appendices
TINCOURT.	22"	11 hours	on their fatigue at ROISEL	
		4 "	to Salvage dump VILLERS-CARBONNEL Collecting timber.	
			R.	
	28"	10 hours	to R.E. dump MONTIGNY for 5th Field Squadron R.E. at O.C. dump.	
		2 "	to ÉQUANCOURT for Q 39th DIV	
	29"		Camps moved to BRAY-SUR-SOMME.	
		5 hours	reported to 333" Canadian CORPS SALLY SALLETS for duty with Field tubes.	
BRAY-SUR-SOMME.	30"	15 hours	on duty with Field tubes, lines fatigue at Reading tubes	
			BRAY-SUR-SOMME.	

O.M.Marshall.
Major.
O.C. 3rd CAV AMM PARK.

WAR DIARY
or
INTELLIGENCE SUMMARY.

(Erase heading not required.)

Ammunition May 1917.

Army Form C. 2118.

Instructions regarding War Diaries and Intelligence Summaries are contained in F. S. Regs., Part II. and the Staff Manual respectively. Title pages will be prepared in manuscript.

Place	Date	Hour	Summary of Events and Information	Remarks and references to Appendices
Receipts				
	1-5-17		O.C. Essex Yeomanry S.A.A .303	20,000 Rnd
	2-5-17		O.C. 10th Royal Hussars S.A.A .303	20,000
	" "		" " " " "	3,000
	2-5-17		O.C. 3rd Dragoon Guards Webley Pistol	1,000
	6-5-17		O.C. 3rd " " " S.A.A .303	10,000
	" "		" " " Ball Ammn. between " "	626
	" "		8th M.G. Squadron " "	626
	" "		" " " S.A.A .303	19,000
	" "		" " " " "	1,000
	7-5-17		O.C. G Bty. R.H.A. S.A.A .303	587
	" "		" " " " Pistol Webley	
	11-6-14	00	Dannies S.A.A 91.363	52,000
	" "		O.C. 8th M.G Squadron S.A.A .303	66,000
	" "	00	Dannies C.P.	2,024
	" "		" C.P.X	672
	" "		D.A. Dos Defective Primers	14
	12-5-17		O.C. Amn. Col. 3rd Cav. Div. Lewis Ammun.1" S.A.A .303	1,000
	23-5-14		O.C. Amn. Sub Park C.P.	450
	" "		" " " " C.P.X.	1,752
	24-5-14		O.C. Essex Yeomanry Mills No.5	952
	" "		" " Signal Flare Gold	108
	" "		" " 4" Bob. Ami Col	360
	" "		" " " "	204

Army Form C. 2118.

WAR DIARY
or
INTELLIGENCE SUMMARY.
(Erase heading not required.)

Instructions regarding War Diaries and Intelligence Summaries are contained in F. S. Regs., Part II. and the Staff Manual respectively. Title pages will be prepared in manuscript.

Place	Date	Hour	Summary of Events and Information	Remarks and references to Appendices

Mileage + Petrol Consumption for May 1917.

            Miles   Petrol (galls)   Miles per Gall

Lorries 14,313   2,459   5.83
Cars   2,181   145   15.0
Cycles   2,182   51   42.60

Vol 29

Confidential.

War Diary

of

3rd Cavalry Ammunition Park.

From 1st June 1917.   to 30th June 1917.

(Volume 29.)

Army Form C. 2118.

WAR DIARY
or
INTELLIGENCE SUMMARY.
(Erase heading not required.)

Instructions regarding War Diaries and Intelligence Summaries are contained in F. S. Regs., Part II. and the Staff Manual respectively. Title pages will be prepared in manuscript.

Place	Date	Hour	Summary of Events and Information	Remarks and references to Appendices
BRAY sur Somme.	1 6/17		Rations drawn from LA FLAQUE.	
"	2 6/17		15 lorries conveying Stores for Road Repairs from BRAY Station to ALBERT–BRAY road detail carried out from BRAY Station.	
"	3 6/17		Same detail.	
"	4 6/17		Same detail.	
"	5 6/17		Five lorries proceeded to No 333 Road Construction Coy RE's at SAILLY. SAILLISEL to relieve five lorries working with above Coy.	
"	6 6/17		Same detail from Bray siding.	
"	6 6/17		One lorry to 4ya Press PERONNE	
"	7 6/17		Same detail from BRAY siding	
"	8 6/17		Same detail from BRAY siding finished.	
"	8 6/17		15 lorries proceeded to Grove TOWN to carry stone to MEAULT–BRAY road	
"	9 6/17		Same detail on MEAULT road	
"	9 6/17		5 lorries proceeded to SAILLY SAILLISEL to replace 5 working there.	
"	10 6/17		Same detail on 9/6/17 to MEAULT. road	
"	11 6/17		Same detail on 10/6/17	

Army Form C. 2118.

WAR DIARY
or
INTELLIGENCE SUMMARY.
(Erase heading not required.)

Instructions regarding War Diaries and Intelligence Summaries are contained in F. S. Regs., Part II. and the Staff Manual respectively. Title pages will be prepared in manuscript.

Place	Date	Hour	Summary of Events and Information	Remarks and references to Appendices
BRAY sur SOMME	12/6/17		Same detail as 11/6/17 finished dump.	
"	13/6/17		15 lorries proceeded to DOMPIERRE to Stone Dump remaining at DOMPIERRE.	
"	14/6/17		Head Qrs of Park remain at BRAY.	
"	15/6/17		5 lorries return from DOMPIERRE and proceed to stone dump at MEAULT.	
"	16/6/17		Same detail as above.	
			One lorry to Tyre Press PERONNE	
	17/6/17		Same detail as 15/6/17.	
	18/6/17		Same detail as 15/6/17	
	19/6/17		Same detail as 15/6/17	
	20/6/17		Same detail as 15/6/17	
	21/6/17		Same detail as 15/6/17	
			One lorry to Tyre Press PERONNE.	
			One lorry to 4th Bde RHA with gun wheels.	
	22/6/17		Lorries returned from DOMPIERRE. remaining details same.	
	23/6/17		10 lorries from BRAY aiding with stone to CAPPY Road.	

Army Form C. 2118.

WAR DIARY
or
INTELLIGENCE SUMMARY.
(Erase heading not required.)

Instructions regarding War Diaries and Intelligence Summaries are contained in F. S. Regs., Part II. and the Staff Manual respectively. Title pages will be prepared in manuscript.

Place	Date	Hour	Summary of Events and Information	Remarks and references to Appendices
BRAY-SUR-SOMME	24/6/17		Same detail as lorries action BEAUXTE.	
	25/6/17		15 lorries to PLATEAU dump	
	26/6/17		Same as 25/6/17	
	27/6/17		Same as 25/6/17	
	28/6/17		Same as 25/6/17	
	29/6/17		Same as 25/6/17	
	30/6/17		Company left BRAY for LE MESNIL. lorries from SAILLY-SAILLISEL returned to Park	

Lorries stores from PLATEAU to PERONNE road

WAR DIARY
or
INTELLIGENCE SUMMARY.
(Erase heading not required.)

Army Form C. 2118.

MILEAGE AND PETROL CONSUMPTION FOR JUNE 1917

	MILES	PETROL (GALLS)	MILES PER GALLON
Lorries	19,406	3118	6.21 approx.
Cars	2,153	134	16.07 "
Cycles	2,494	53½	46.61 "

Army Form C. 2118.

WAR DIARY
or
INTELLIGENCE SUMMARY.
(Erase heading not required.)

Ammunition June 1917

Instructions regarding War Diaries and Intelligence Summaries are contained in F. S. Regs., Part II. and the Staff Manual respectively. Title pages will be prepared in manuscript.

Place	Date	Hour	Summary of Events and Information	Remarks and references to Appendices
			Receipts	
			Nil	
			Issues	
			Nil	

Vol 30.

Confidential

War Diary

of

3rd Cavalry Ammunition Park.

From 1st July 1917 to 31st July 1917.

Volume 30.

Army Form C. 2118.

WAR DIARY
or
INTELLIGENCE SUMMARY.
(Erase heading not required.)

Instructions regarding War Diaries and Intelligence Summaries are contained in F. S. Regs., Part II. and the Staff Manual respectively. Title pages will be prepared in manuscript.

Place	Date	Hour	Summary of Events and Information	Remarks and references to Appendices
LE MESNIL	1/7/17		12 Gunners on Steves fatigue at Brig Station. 1 Army Service Corps to 6th Bde H.Q. to remain until further required	
"	2/7/17		12 Gunners on Steves fatigue at Brig Station. 1 " " " to 6th Bde H.Q. 1 " " 7th " " } to remain until further is required	
"	3/7/17		Return Gunner to Div H.Q. for duty during truce. 12 " on Steves fatigue at Brig Station. 1 " to H.Q. A.S.C. during truce.	
"	4/7/17		1 Car Gunner to O.C. A.S.C. for duty during truce. Le-France. Light exchange to Car and horses. 12 Gunners on Steves fatigue at Brig Station.	
"	5/7/17		12 Gunners on Steves fatigue at Brig Station.	

Army Form C. 2118.

WAR DIARY
or
INTELLIGENCE SUMMARY.

(Erase heading not required.)

Instructions regarding War Diaries and Intelligence Summaries are contained in F. S. Regs., Part II. and the Staff Manual respectively. Title pages will be prepared in manuscript.

Place	Date	Hour	Summary of Events and Information	Remarks and references to Appendices
LE MENSIL	6.7.17		12 hours on Gen. fatigue at BRIE &Ltd.	
"	7.7.17		" " " " " "	
"	8.7.17		" " " " " "	
"	9.7.17		" " " " " "	
"	10.7.17		No detail.	
"	11.7.17		10 hours to ammn dump at HANCOURT loaded and returned.	
"	12.7.17		No detail.	
"	13.7.17		6 Corps lorries to Cav Corps Camp ammn dump for 1 days duty. 2 " to Tyre pres at PERONNE.	

2353 Wt. W2544/1454 700,000 5/15 D. D. & L. A.D.S.S./Forms/C. 2118.

Army Form C. 2118.

WAR DIARY
or
INTELLIGENCE SUMMARY.
(Erase heading not required.)

Instructions regarding War Diaries and Intelligence Summaries are contained in F. S. Regs., Part II. and the Staff Manual respectively. Title pages will be prepared in manuscript.

Place	Date	Hour	Summary of Events and Information	Remarks and references to Appendices
LE MENSIL	14.7.17		12 Lorries to Can Corps for 1 day duty. Lorries april 2.0 ordered to Pernes Etaples.	
"	15.7.17		Lys. LE MENSIL at 6.50 am arrived PERNES at 5.0 pm	
PERNES	16.7.17		1 lorry to Tin Pin for ISBERGES 7 lorries to LAPOONOY to pick up Chinamen from 4th & 6th Div. and convey to HAVERSKERQUE. 5 lorries to MARLES to Censer "	
"	17.7.17		Left PERNES at 9.0 am arrived HOLANDERIE at 11.50 am 1 lorry to Repark Killers to convey Rail Lengths to Div.	
HOLANDERIE	18.7.17		4 lorries to BERGUETTE to convey China 6th Regiment 1 " to Repark Lillers to convey Rail Lengths to 7th Div.	

2353 Wt. W2544/1454 700,000 5/15 D. D. & L. A.D.S.S./Forms/C. 2118.

WAR DIARY
or
INTELLIGENCE SUMMARY.

(Erase heading not required.)

Army Form C. 2118.

Place	Date	Hour	Summary of Events and Information	Remarks and references to Appendices
HOLANDERIE	19.7.17		One lorry to Salvage at AIRE and returning with stores.	
"	20.7.17	3 lorries	took to the Brigade returning to Park.	
		1 "	to LILLERS Station with party 7" L.A.M.B. to handle stores	
"	21.7.17		Nil.	
"	22.7.17	1 lorry	to 1st Cav Divn Park to deliver ammunition	
"	23.7.17	7 lorries	to BRUAY to carry coal ad chalum ordre ??? 7. D.S.O.	
		1 "	to BOURECQ 7th Regiment. Group d'Armeny Ramps a d Pengh	
"	24.7.17	18 lorries	Conveyed troops to Trening School DAMNES.	
"	25.7.17	2 lorries	reported to D.S.O. BUSNES returning ??? to 7" Regt.	

WAR DIARY
INTELLIGENCE SUMMARY

Army Form C. 2118.

Place	Date	Hour	Summary of Events and Information	Remarks and references to Appendices
HOLLANDSCHE	26/7/17		2 Lorries to 3rd Field Squadron R.E. Evening Machine Gun Layer 1 Lorry reported to G.S. Officer DIV HQ to establish dumps to Brigade.	
"	27/7/17		nil	
"	28/7/17		One Lorry reported to H.Q. Royal Engineers Estate party to Tramway School at 7pm 1700 hrs. Proceeded to OUDTON for working party 2 NC 6th DIV	
"	29/7/17		1 Lorry to DAMMES lorries Park at disposal there until down on 24 E	
"	30/7/17		nil	
"	31/7/17		nil	

D.O.D. Mitchell
Major

Army Form C. 2118.

WAR DIARY
or
INTELLIGENCE SUMMARY.
(Erase heading not required.)

MILEAGE AND PETROL CONSUMPTION FOR JULY 1917.

	MILES	PETROL (GALLS)	MILES PER GALLON
LORRIES	16,123	2546½	6.29
CARS	2,312	151	15.31
CYCLES	3,368	80	42.10

Army Form C. 2118

WAR DIARY
or
INTELLIGENCE SUMMARY

(Erase heading not required.) Ammunition for July 1917.

Instructions regarding War Diaries and Intelligence Summaries are contained in F. S. Regs., Part II. and the Staff Manual respectively. Title Pages will be prepared in manuscript.

Place	Date	Hour	Summary of Events and Information	Remarks and references to Appendices
	16-7-17	D.I. 1.13 pm	Receipts	
	do	N.X.	1752	
			944	
			Issues	
			25-4-16 "K" Rty Bow N — 19
			26-7-92 "Q" " I " — 1
			30-7-16 Am Col 3rd Can Div N 3

Vol 31

Confidential

War Diary

of

3rd Cavalry Ammunition Park

From 1st August 1914 to 31st August 1914.

Volume 31.

Army Form C. 2118.

WAR DIARY
or
INTELLIGENCE SUMMARY.
(Erase heading not required.)

Instructions regarding War Diaries and Intelligence Summaries are contained in F. S. Regs., Part II. and the Staff Manual respectively. Title pages will be prepared in manuscript.

Place	Date	Hour	Summary of Events and Information	Remarks and references to Appendices
HOLLEBEKE	1.8.17		Nil.	
"	2nd		One lorry to R.E. Park LILLERS and delivered Stores to 7th Bde.	
			Fore lim to ORD Walker WESTOUTRE to draw a 2 return Same to	
			One lorry to S.A. School DAMNES to bring back lorry to Wizad	
"	3rd		One lorry delivered ammunt to Wizad	
			One " to Tyre from at ISBERGUES	
"	4th		One lorry to ammn Col Armaments at ST FLORIS	
"	5th		One lorry to R.E. dump at K.S. B.S. 3 Sheet 36B Collect Stores &	
			Complete Return a 2 Return to depar to	
			One lorry to BUSNES picked up drivers and ran a 2 lots to Callest	

Army Form C. 2118.

WAR DIARY
or
INTELLIGENCE SUMMARY.
(Erase heading not required.)

Instructions regarding War Diaries and Intelligence Summaries are contained in F. S. Regs., Part II. and the Staff Manual respectively. Title pages will be prepared in manuscript.

Place	Date	Hour	Summary of Events and Information	Remarks and references to Appendices
HOLLANDERIE	6		One lorry to 7th Bde field of fire. One lorry to Remount hay on OUDEZEM. Two lorries to HAZEBROUCK and carrying parts to ROMBLY.	
"	7		One lorry to Div Hqrs demp. One lorry Glen to 7th A.B. Two lorries to WESTHOEK at elim to 21st V.A.A.	
"	8			
"	9		Nil	
"	10		One lorry to Main Cat not arrived.	
"	11		One lorry to ROMBLY allur Glen at 2 return to BOSNES	
"	12		One lorry to HAZEBROUCK take dny 2nd Royal Dragoons. One lorry to Amm Col not arrived. One lorry to WESTOUTRE OKO allur + flour at chiluch lagemens	

T2134. Wt. W708—776. 500000. 4/15. Sir J. C. & S.

Army Form C. 2118.

WAR DIARY
or
INTELLIGENCE SUMMARY.
(Erase heading not required.)

Instructions regarding War Diaries and Intelligence Summaries are contained in F.S. Regs., Part II and the Staff Manual respectively. Title pages will be prepared in manuscript.

Place	Date	Hour	Summary of Events and Information	Remarks and references to Appendices
HOOGRAAF	13		Nil	
"	14		Nil	
"	15		One lorry to DICKEBOSCH for rations for the Regt	
"	16		One lorry to O.R.D. Railhead to collect flour and chloride of lime	
"	16		One lorry to WESTOUTRE for rations	
"	17		Two lorries to 5th Cav Mun Park 2.0.d.17.32 2.5.7. N.armcmt at AIX NOULETTE	
"	18		One lorry to 2nd Cav Amn Park for supplies at GOUY-EN-TOURNAISE	
"	18		One lorry to O.R.D. for ammunition	
"	19		Two lorries to LE SART and LE CORBIE to take over parks and ammunition	

T2134. Wt. W708—776. 500000. 4/15. Sir J.C. & S.

Army Form C. 2118.

WAR DIARY
or
INTELLIGENCE SUMMARY.
(Erase heading not required.)

Instructions regarding War Diaries and Intelligence Summaries are contained in F. S. Regs., Part II. and the Staff Manual respectively. Title pages will be prepared in manuscript.

Place	Date	Hour	Summary of Events and Information	Remarks and references to Appendices
HOULNOEIC	20		Nil	
"	21st		Orderly to MINRE and to stores and delivered to LEDRINGHEM & HAYERSKERQUE. Two runs to Brigade Field Officer.	
"	22		Orderly to REPAIR SHEDS HAYERSKERQUE. Some runs to LEDRINGHEM and Officers as ordered to HAM-IN-ARTOIS. Orderly to Forage Officer LA MOTTE AUX BOIS and taken to GORRISQUE	
"	23		Orderly to and from Div Chaunce officer BOSNES. Orderly to and from Camp Commandant Div HQ	
"	24		Orderly to and from Div HQ. Orderly to REPAIR SHEDS to obtain Orderlies to BOSEGHEM. Orderly to WITTERNESSE & bring Orderlies back carrying material to Div HQ	
"	25		Orderly to Pipe and all Field Services 3rd Cav Div	

WAR DIARY
or
INTELLIGENCE SUMMARY.
(Erase heading not required.)

Army Form C. 2118.

Place	Date	Hour	Summary of Events and Information	Remarks and references to Appendices
HAZEBROUCK	26"		First man down to bathe one cavalry horse to blacksmith	
"	27"		One lorry to DIV HQ to duty.	
			One lorry to DRANVILLE, SAA Col down to Fourn Col at LE SART	
"	28"		One lorry to Reg Pros ISBERGUES	
			Four lorries on duty to DIV H.Q. to transport personnel.	
			One lorry better R15 at DOMPIERRE as return to HAZEVENTE	
			One lorry to DN to collect stuff, & return to HQ Lorries.	
			One lorry to Refal Divers collect stores & return to BOESEGHEM	
"	29"		Two men down to bathe one cavalry horse to blacksmith	
			One lorry to BOESEGHEM with flour	
			One lorry to PERRIER a warr. officer and into to NOEUX-LES-MINES.	
			Two lorries to 2nd RB to pick up troops & take & HQ & farm on 30 Coy	
			10 fatigue men duty horse & cavalry horse to blacksmith	

Army Form C. 2118.

WAR DIARY
or
INTELLIGENCE SUMMARY.
(Erase heading not required.)

Place	Date	Hour	Summary of Events and Information	Remarks and references to Appendices
MOURMELON	30th		Strength 6 Officers APO & NCOs 86 to 3 Wagons Our tent taken to Camp Hampshire for our TRONPY at fields	
	31st		Belong to OKD walked with Lieuremants Officers Two men to Town in Relief of Brothers	

[signature]
Major

Army Form C. 2118.

WAR DIARY
or
INTELLIGENCE SUMMARY.

(Erase heading not required.)

Instructions regarding War Diaries and Intelligence Summaries are contained in F. S. Regs., Part II. and the Staff Manual respectively. Title pages will be prepared in manuscript.

Place	Date	Hour	Summary of Events and Information	Remarks and references to Appendices
			Seen copy of mileage and petrol consumption for August 1917.	
			mileage	total expended.
			6002	4005
				5.93
			3046	175	17.4
			39110	66	144.54

2353 Wt. W2544/1454 700,000 5/15 D. D. & L. A.D.S.S./Forms/C. 2118.

Army Form C. 2118.

WAR DIARY
or
INTELLIGENCE SUMMARY.
(Erase heading not required.)

Instructions regarding War Diaries and Intelligence Summaries are contained in F. S. Regs., Part II. and the Staff Manual respectively. Title pages will be prepared in manuscript.

Ammn. August 1917

Place	Date	Hour	Summary of Events and Information	Remarks and references to Appendices
			Receipts	Issues
2/8/17	S.A.A. 303 Ball O.K.D		303,000	2/8/17 S.A.A. 303 D.T. Army G/S	90,000
-do-	Cart. Illum. 1" O.K. expo		12	-do- -do- 6" Ammn. Col	283,000
-do-	Gren. Hand 203 O.K.D		2560	7/8/17 -do- -do-	60,000
-do-	Pistol Webby O.K.D		13512	9/8/17 -do- -do-	17,000
12-8-17	Gren. Hand 203 O.K.D		256	11/8/17 -do- -do-	21,000
18-8-17	Shrapnel N PESELHOEK		1732	2/8/17 Pistol Webby -do-	13512
22-8-17	S.A.A. 303 4th M.G. Sqdn		35000	12/8/17 Shrapnel N 5th Cav Am Col	1732
24-8-17	S.A.A 303 arras		440000	26/8/17 S.A.A. 303 Am Col	25,000
				29/8/17 -do- -do-	440,000

T2134. Wt. W708—776. 500000. 4/15. Sir J. C. & S.

Vol 32

Confidential.
War Diary.
of
3rd Cavalry Ammunition Park.
From 1st September 1917 to 30th September 1917

Volume 32.

3rd CAVALRY AMMN. PARK.

Sept 1917

Army Form C. 2118.

WAR DIARY
or
INTELLIGENCE SUMMARY.
(Erase heading not required.)

Place	Date	Hour	Summary of Events and Information	Remarks and references to Appendices
			Mileage and Petrol consumption for September 1917.	copy
			Mileage. Petrol consumed. miles per gallon.	
			Lorries 4260. 697. 16.11	
			Cars - 2723. 150. 18.15	
			Motor Cycles 2341. 46. 50.89	

3rd CAVALRY AMMN. PARK.
Sept 1917

Army Form C. 2118.

WAR DIARY
or
INTELLIGENCE SUMMARY
(Erase heading not required.)

Place	Date	Hour	Summary of Events and Information	Remarks and references to Appendices
HOUDANGRIE	1.9.17		4 lorries returned empty to PRONAY.	
"	2 "		to Rucklands for supply lorries of S.A.A.	
"	3 "		3 lorries returned empty to 7th Div from GARBECQUE to new area.	
"			1 " to PRONAY into lines.	
"	4 "		1 lorry to PERNES as chauffeur to ambulance ammunition.	
"			6 " to BUSNES for Tour troops.	
"	5 "		1 lorry to R.E. dump thro 36 B. K.s. 13. S. 3. between Olers.	
"	6 "		1 lorry cleaned, signed thro dump at TREPIED.	
"	7 "		7 lorries to Tour troops BUSNES to fetch slag to roads.	0000
"	8 "		Nil	

3 / 8rd CAVALRY AMMN. PARK
Sept 1917

Army Form C. 2118.

WAR DIARY
or
INTELLIGENCE SUMMARY
(Erase heading not required.)

Instructions regarding War Diaries and Intelligence Summaries are contained in F. S. Regs., Part II. and the Staff Manual respectively. Title pages will be prepared in manuscript.

Place	Date	Hour	Summary of Events and Information	Remarks and references to Appendices
HOLLANDTIE	8		nil	
"	9		nil	
"	10		nil	
"	11		1 lorry moving this between PIERNES and RANG-DU-FLIERS.	
"	12		nil	
"	13		nil	
"	14		nil	
"	15		1 lorry from daily to PERNES	2000

4

3rd CAVALRY AMMN. PARK.
Sep/917

Army Form C. 2118.

Instructions regarding War Diaries and Intelligence
Summaries are contained in F. S. Regs., Part II.
and the Staff Manual respectively. Title pages
will be prepared in manuscript.

WAR DIARY
or
INTELLIGENCE SUMMARY.
(Erase heading not required.)

Place	Date	Hour	Summary of Events and Information	Remarks and references to Appendices
HOUDAIN	16th		11 Lorries from BUSNES to ticker flag.	
"	17th		1 Lorry to RANG-DU-FLIERS to carry stores for Divisional Yeomanry, 1 " to RE Yard BETHUNE to change horse lines.	
"	18th		Ditto	
"	19th		Ditto	
"	20th		Ditto	
"	21st		Ditto	
"	22nd		1 lorry to R.E. Yard Lillers to clear Lorry lines.	
"	23rd		2 lorries on duty 24 to 10 "HRs, to depart to ECHINGHEN.	○○○○○

T2134. Wt. W708—776. 500000. 4/15. Sir J. C. & S.

3rd CAVALRY AMMN. PARK.
Apr 1917

Army Form C. 2118.

WAR DIARY
or
INTELLIGENCE SUMMARY.
(Erase heading not required.)

Place	Date	Hour	Summary of Events and Information	Remarks and references to Appendices
HESDIGNEUL	24th		2 lorries on duty with 57th C.C.S. bearing Christmas from to VENANT then ARRAS.	
"	25th		6 " " " " " " " " " " ARRAS	
"	26th		1 " " " " " " " " " "	
			1 lorry to 8th Bde to carry party to AIRE	
			1 " to Advance AIRE	
			3 lorries on Amm duty	
			1 lorry to 6th Bde to take party to ECHINGHEN near BOULOGNE	
"	27th		3 lorries on Amm duty	
			O.C. P.S.C. inspected this Unit.	
			Lights(?) car sent to PREVENT to collect before bombs etc a [?] deliver to Bde	
"	28th		3 lorries on duty with Front Division attached to 6 DIV	
			1 lorry to RE yard Lillers. Hunes(?) bringing a lorries to Regt.	

3rd CAVALRY AMMN. PARK.

Sept 1917

WAR DIARY
or
INTELLIGENCE SUMMARY.

Army Form C. 2118.

Place	Date	Hour	Summary of Events and Information	Remarks and references to Appendices
HOUTKERQUE	29		2 lorries on duty with Reserve Park to FLORIS. 3 " " " " to "57" C.C.S. 1 lorry to Q.A.GORGE for timber	
"	30		8 lorries detailed to carry men & kits of dismounted parties from YPRES area to various map references	

J.M.M. Winfield
Major

WAR DIARY
or
INTELLIGENCE SUMMARY.

Army Form C. 2118.

3rd CAVALRY AMMN. PARK.
Sept 1917

Place	Date	Hour	Summary of Events and Information	Remarks and references to Appendices
			Ammn. September 1917	
			Receipts Issues	
3-9-17	Ammn. bol. S.A.A. 303	60,000	3-9-17 To 7th M.G. Squadron S.A.A. 303	44,000
26-9-17	Ammn. col. S.A.A. 303	26,000	3-9-17 To 1st Life Guards S.A.A. 303	2,204
24-9-17	1st Battery Rds N	58	8-9-17 Do Review Geo S.A.A. 303	2,204
			9-9-17 To Brent Bugs S.A.A. 303	2,000
			" Do — Amb Welly	467
			26-9-17 To "K" Battery Rds N.Shyffus	227
			" Do No -	12.4
			" Do — N.X. — A.B.	—
			" To 2nd Life Guards S.A.A. 303	2,204
			" To 1st Life Guards S.A.A. 303	16,000
			24-9-17 To "K" Battery Rds N.Shyffus	10,000
				58

J.M. Mitchell Capt

Confidential.

War Diary.

of

16th Company H.S.E. (M.S.)

From 1st October 1917 to 31st October 1917.

Volume 33.

Army Form C. 2118.

WAR DIARY
or
INTELLIGENCE SUMMARY.

(Erase heading not required.)

3rd Cav Train Paul.
76th Co DAC
Army of October 1917

Place	Date	Hour	Summary of Events and Information	Remarks and references to Appendices
HOULINGHEM	1/11		On leave from 6am C Bourne	
	2		4 men to 53 CCS to train, that 76 TMDAC	
	3			
	4		2 am on Armo duty	
	5		1 am on Armo duty	
	6		2 am to Army for fatigue to kill 6 bullock	
			1 am to Econ reinforcemt of 1 Cav & Hyba	
	7		Officer on duty 1 Lieut G.F.O. Kempton for 6.0. Compy	

Army Form C. 2118.

WAR DIARY
or
INTELLIGENCE SUMMARY.

3rd Cav. Div. Pearl.
76th Co. D.J.C.
(Erase heading not required).

Army from October 1917.

Place	Date	Hour	Summary of Events and Information	Remarks and references to Appendices
FOLLENVILLE	8		[illegible with Tp.]	
"	9		Cyclist to BAPAUME to fetch Mounts.	
			3 Lorries Ammn. dump to LESART	
			2 " 6o LESART Convoys troops to BUSNES.	
			1 Lorry to VERMANT coll. Ammn. Supplies.	
"	10		1 Lorry 6o LESART Ammn. to 8th Bde.	
			1 " to PERNES Conveying Ammn. dups. to Life Guards. & 1 R. Hus.G. R.H.A.	
			3 Lorries to Convoy Ammn. dups. from DIEVRE to COLLORE	
"	11		1 Lorry to Ammn. dump from 8 Bde.	
			2 Lorries on Ammn. duty from PEPPRINGHE to LESART	
			6o CAMBLAIN to take Ammn. dups. to MARIST & O MERVILLE.	
			2 " 6o LESART a.f. LEPARACIE FARM	
			1 " Ammn. duty 6o LESART a.f. LEPARACIE FARM	

2353 Wt W25H/1454 700,000 5/15 D. D. & L. A.D.S.S./Forms/C. 2118.

Army Form C. 2118.

WAR DIARY
or
INTELLIGENCE SUMMARY.

(Erase heading not required.)

3rd Chev[?] [?] Part.
26 to DVR
Training for October 1917.

No. 3

Instructions regarding War Diaries and Intelligence Summaries are contained in F. S. Regs., Part II. and the Staff Manual respectively. Title pages will be prepared in manuscript.

Place	Date	Hour	Summary of Events and Information	Remarks and references to Appendices
HOUDAIN	12"		3 am to field stables for Tour Rays in BUSNES.	
			2 " Arm Unity Le SART to LE CORNET MALO	
			1 " Sqn " to MOULIN LE COMTE	
			1 " " to LA COUCHE int[?] RE Glen.	
			1 " ulguns at 15 BERGUES.	
"	13"		2 am Convoys hops from ST FLORIS to talk at BUSNES.	
			3 am Convoys from to ST VENANT.	
			6 " " to AIX NOULETTE	
			8 " to CROIX DE POPERINGHE every time return to F.S.D. BETHUNE 10"	
"	15"		Ams E am included fine return at BETHUNE as what to St Paul.	
			2 am to COLONNE feed at hops at late to PITIN near BAILLEUL.	
			1 leng to Amm GR.	

OC[?]

WAR DIARY or INTELLIGENCE SUMMARY

Army Form C. 2118.

3rd Can[adian] Sanitary Sect[ion]
76. C.D.S.S.

Place	Date	Hour	Summary of Events and Information	Remarks and references to Appendices
FOUQUEREUIL	16"	8 am	to DOULLENS to unload fruit.	
	17"	3 "	to Div HQ. BUSNES for ammo. to new area.	
		5 "	to Bde HQ. nr RUE DE GARBECQUE moving to new area.	
		4 "	to BRUAY to unload and return to Supply Col at Relay for same.	
		1 am	to A.D.M.S. BUSNES for issue.	
		1 "	" O.C. A.S.C. " "	
		1 "	to Tpn near BERGUETTE	
		3 am	to CROIX DE POPERINGHE for gum rubber.	
	18"	2 am	to BETHUNE. (F.S.D.) Iron — gum rubber.	
		3 "	to ST VENANT rat[ion] dump.	
		4 "	to ROBECQ " "	
		5 "	to LES LAURIERS to move 6" Bde to new area.	
	19"	1 Lorry	sent from Supply to ST VENANT.	
		1 "	" gum rubber from REEFERS to Town large BUSNES.	

WAR DIARY or INTELLIGENCE SUMMARY

(Erase heading not required.)

Army Form C. 2118.

3rd Cav. Arm. Park.
76th Co DSC
from 20th October 1917

Place	Date	Hour	Summary of Events and Information	Remarks and references to Appendices
HORNOVE	20		5 lorries issued 8" Bde from PRESSY SACHIN to their own H. to BRUAY to draw Ord.cl. & return to Offly CR.	
" "	21		Honoured 7, 76 Co DSC consists of the following O.C. Major Blundell Lce Farrier, M.S.M. C.S.M. C.Q.M.S. 2 Sergts, 2 return & 1 on Cpl on loan from Hunts depot, from ABBEVILLE to report to D.D.T. (S). The lorry & transport with all vehicles handed over by a dm. of 3rd Cav. Div Q. to Capt. McCullum as Cav-Offrs.s	
ABBEVILLE	22		Staying at ABBEVILLE. Orders received from D.D.T. (S) that the whole of 3rd Cav. Arm. Park, 76th Coy DSC to be the nucleus of a G.H.Q. Reserve M.T. Co and to retain old Co number.	
" "	23		Received 1 Thornycroft lorry-car two lorries & two blue lorries and left for St VALERY SUR SOMME. Three Cos also formed.	

Army Form C. 2118.

G.H.Q. Reserve M.T. Co.
76th Co. P.S.T.
Diary for October 1917

WAR DIARY
or
INTELLIGENCE SUMMARY.
(Erase heading not required.)

Place	Date	Hour	Summary of Events and Information	Remarks and references to Appendices
ST VALERY SUR SOMME	24th		Nil.	
" "	25th		71 - 3 ton lorries formed from 13th Corps H.A.	
" "	26th		Nil.	
" "	27th		1 lorry to type Pero ABBEVILLE.	
" "	28th		1 lorry on empty duty ret. 36th Co P.S.T. St VALERY.	
" "	29th		1 lorry to D.O.R.E. NOYELLE to return fairs - 2 x R.E. Dunbains to Corbens ELP.	
" "			1 " to ABBEVILLE to Corbens Stern c.s farm Forbes	
" "	30th		1 lorry to D.O.R.E. as in do 29th.	

WAR DIARY
or
INTELLIGENCE SUMMARY.

Army Form C. 2118.

G.H.Q. Reserve M.T. Co.
76th Co. A.S.C.
Army to October 1917

Place	Date	Hour	Summary of Events and Information	Remarks and references to Appendices
St VALERY.	31st	11 a.m.	Transferred to 1st M.T. Depot.	
		16 men	" " 56th Co A.S.C.	
		27 "	" " 79th Co A.S.C.	
		45 men	Received from 56th Co & 79th Co A.S.C.	

J.D.D. Mitchell
Major
O.C. G.H.Q. Reserve M.T. Co.
76th Co A.S.C.

31/10/17.